WHAT OTHERS HAVE SAID ABOUT SENATOR HARRY REID

"Harry Reid is a fighter. In his five terms as a U.S. Senator, Harry has fought for good jobs, a safer environment for our kids, and affordable health care for all. He's never backed down from tough decisions or been afraid to choose what is right over what is easy. Time and again, Harry stood up to special interests and made sure every one of his constituents had a voice in their nation's capital."

President Barack Obama

"From humble beginnings in Searchlight to the United States Senate, Senator Reid's story is one that represents the Nevada and American dream."

Nevada Governor Brian Sandoval

"Harry Reid has been the most effective fighter the state of Nevada has ever had in the United States Senate."

The Nevada State Democratic Party

somebody

harry reid's journey

forgot

from searchlight

to tell

to spotlight

harry

adrienne tropp

Lucky Bat Books

A Lucky Bat Book

Somebody Forgot to Tell Harry

Cover Artist: Nuno Moreira

ISBN 978-1-943588-12-1

Published by Lucky Bat Books

10 9 8 7 6 5 4 3 2 1

ACKNOWLEDGEMENTS

Many hands, invisible to the reader, have been behind *Somebody Forgot to Tell Harry*. The idea for the biography came from Suzanne Morgan Williams, my mentor at the Society of Children's Book Writers and Illustrators (SC-BWI) who motivated me to begin. My friend Virginia Castlemen has offered her valuable advice when I've had questions. Editing by Chris Eboch and Carol Purroy was valuable in helping focus the manuscript. Without Jessica Santina, who answered my endless questions and fine-tuned the manuscript, *Somebody Forgot to Tell Harry* would never have been published. The unwavering encouragement of my children and their spouses and my friends kept up my enthusiasm for the project. My husband, Richard, remained at my side offering whatever was necessary: chauffeur, photographer, and proofreader. Any mistakes that remain, I blame on my less-than-eagle eyes. A thank you to all.

Adrienne

To Ricky, who supports all that I do.

CONTENTS

TIMELINE   i

INTRODUCTION   vii

PART 1: BEGINNINGS

Searchlight: Where Few Want to Live   1

A Hard Life in a Small Town   5

Fighting at Home and Beyond   12

From Searchlight and Back Again   16

Almost Arrested   23

A Different World Outside Searchlight   25

PART 2: MONEY STRUGGLES

High School and Better Times   33

And More School   43

Another Route?   45

An Elopement   47

Life as a Married Man   49

Money Problems and More Money Problems   52

PART 3: AT LAST, THE WORKING WORLD

Making a Name for Himself   57

Was It Murder?   64

A Try at Elected Office   71

Winning and Losing   73

The FBI, Ex-Texas Rangers, Gangsters, and Bomb Threats   82

PART 4: D.C., ANOTHER TRY?

Back to Washington   89

Important Jobs and Trouble   102

Becoming the Most Important Senator   105

Reid's Politics   112

Success for Others   113

Some of Harry's Other Interests and Views   116

Our Words Are Important   121

Out to Get Him   124

Then Came the Election of 2014: Did They Get Him?   129

Health Issues   132

Landra, Harry, and Family   135

A Surprise?   137

The American Dream?   140

GOVERNMENT TERMS USED IN *SOMEBODY FORGOT TO TELL HARRY*   142

BIBLIOGRAPHY   148

PHOTO CREDITS   161

INDEX   169

ABOUT THE AUTHOR   183

FIGURES

Figure 1: "Map of World's Largest Deserts."   1

Figure 2: Richard Tropp. "Searchlight, Nevada."   2

Figure 3: Ian Macky. "Map of Nevada (with Searchlight)."   7

Figure 4: Richard Tropp. Elementary school Reid attended   8

Figure 5: Richard Tropp. The current Reid Elementary School in Searchlight, Nevada   8

Figure 6: The home where Harry Reid grew up.   9

Figure 7: "Wounded soldiers in a trench."   18

Figure 8: "U.S. soldiers take cover under fire somewhere in Germany."   18

Figure 9: "U.S. Marines operating an M1919 A4 during World War II."   19

Figure 10: Jurgen Stroop Report to Heinrich Himmler from May 1943.   19

Figure 11: "Coutances, France: one of many destroyed towns."   19

Figure 12: Charles Levy. "Mushroom cloud from the atomic explosion over Nagasaki at 11:02 a.m., August 9, 1945."   20

Figure 13: "Nagasaki, Japan following the atomic bombing on August 9, 1945."   20

Figure 14: Harry Reid, Sr. (age 2) in 1916 with family.   21

Figure 15: "Jackie Robinson and Branch Rickey sign the contract that broke baseball's color barrier, August 28, 1945."   27

Figure 16: Bob Sandberg. "Robinson in Dodgers uniform, 1954."   27

Figure 17: "Jackie Robinson sliding onto base."   28

Figure 18: "Congressional Gold Medal awarded to Jackie Robinson."   28

Figure 19: "The two Koreas, split at the 38th Parallel."   37

Figure 20: "United Nations' forces at the 38th Parallel, retreating back to the south from Pyongyang, in 1950."   38

Figure 21: "Pfc. Julias Van Den Stock of Company A, 32nd Regimental   38

Figure 22: "Men of the 1st Cavalry Division fighting in a train yard in Pyongyang, Korea."   38

Figure 23: Harry Reid in law school   53

Figure 24: Dave Parker. "Nevada Legislature Building, Carson City. Nov. 1, 2007."   72

Figure 25: Lieutenant Governor Harry Reid.   73

Figure 26: "Muhammad Ali."   76

Figure 27: Ira Rosenberg. "Portrait of Muhammad Ali, 1967."   76

Figure 28: "Muhammad Ali (right) fights Joe Frazier."   77

Figure 29: "Rare bristlecone pine at Great Basin National Park."   90

Figure 30: "Wheeler Peak, the tallest peak in Nevada, is inside Great Basin National Park."   91

Figure 31: "Parachute Shield, the most famous shield in Lehman Caves."   91

Figure 32: "Column and drapery formations found in Lehman Caves."   92

Figure 33: "An abundance of speleothems are revealed in each room of Lehman Caves."   92

Figure 34: "Helictites defying gravity, in the West Room of Lehman Caves."   92

Figure 35: "Stalagmite ornately decorated in Lehman Caves."   93

Figure 36: "A rare moment when water is forced under pressure through a soda straw formation."   93

Figure 37: "On rare occasions, bubbles appear on soda straws for a short period of time, usually in early spring."   93

Figure 38: "The emblem of the National Park Service."   95

Figure 39: "Scene at the Signing of the Constitution of the United States."   97

Figure 40: "Kids.gov Three Branches of Government Poster."   98

Figures 41-47: Various pictures of Harry Reid throughout his career.   130

Figure 48: Senator Reid, at his Thursday Breakfast with the public.   131

Figure 49: "Senator Harry Reid meets with Julian Castro, nominee for Secretary of Housing and Urban Development, in July 2014."   131

Figure 50: "President Barack Obama talks with Senator Reid while on Air Force One."   131

Figure 51: Landra Reid.   133

Figure 52: "Harry and Landra Reid with their four sons and daughter."   135

Harry Reid
born
December 2

On September 3, World War II begins

U.S. President is Franklin D. Roosevelt

1950

'53 Heads to high school in Henderson
'55 Elected treasurer at Basic High
'56 Elected senior class president
Dec. 7 on front page of *Las Vegas Sun*
'57 Graduates from Basic High School
'59 Graduates Southern Utah State College
September 12, marries Landra Gould

'55 First McDonald's opens in Illinois

Disneyland opens

'56 Elvis Presley's first hit

First hard disk invented by IBM

'59 Alaska and Hawaii become states

Barbie doll first sold

First pictures of Earth taken by Explorer 6

Xerox copiers for offices

1960

'61 Daughter Lana is born
Graduates from Utah State
'62 Son Rory is born
'61 - '64 Police officer in U.S. Capitol
'63 Admitted to Nevada Bar Association
'64 - '66 Henderson city attorney
'68 Son Leif is born
Elected Nevada state assemblyman

'60   John F. Kennedy elected first Catholic president

'61   Lego blocks first sold in U.S.

Pampers, first disposable diaper, sold

'62   90% of U.S. homes have TVs

'63   President Kennedy assassinated on Nov. 22 and Lyndon B. Johnson becomes president

'64   Civil Rights Act becomes law

Dr. Martin Luther King receives Nobel Peace Prize

'65   Voting Rights Act allows African-Americans over 21 to vote

Russians walk in space

'67   First Super Bowl

Dr. Barnard performs heart transplant

911 Emergency telephone service begins

'68   Dr. King assassinated on April 4

'69   Neil Armstrong walks on moon

Sesame Street goes on the air

1970

'70 Becomes Lieutenant Governor
'71 Son Josh is born
'72 Father commits suicide
'74 Son Key is born
Loses Senate election to Paul Laxalt
'77 - '81 Becomes Chair of Nevada Gaming Commission
'78 Hearing on which *Casino* is based takes place

'71   Voting age lowered to 18 in U.S.

'72   Last U.S. troops leave Vietnam

Arab terrorists murder 11 Olympic athletes

'74   Horrible famine in Africa because of drought

Pocket calculators go on sale

Bar codes first used on products

President Nixon forced to resign and Gerald Ford becomes president

'77   Jimmy Carter elected President

Star Wars movie hits screens

Apple II Computers go on sale

'78   John Paul I becomes Pope, dies, and John Paul II becomes pope 33 days later

Cell phones go on sale

People buy first computer video games

'79   Snowboard invented

Iran became an Islamic Republic and 63 Americans become hostages

1980

'82 Elected to United States House of Representatives
'83 - '87 Serves in House
'86 Elected senator

'80   Ronald Reagan elected president

'81   First flight of Columbia space shuttle

      IBM's first PC

'84   First Macintosh goes on sale

'85   Microsoft and first Windows computer

'87   Simpsons on T.V.

'89   Berlin Wall comes down, uniting Germany

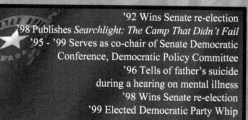

1990

'92 Wins Senate re-election
'98 Publishes *Searchlight: The Camp That Didn't Fail*
'95 - '99 Serves as co-chair of Senate Democratic Conference, Democratic Policy Committee
'96 Tells of father's suicide during a hearing on mental illness
'98 Wins Senate re-election
'99 Elected Democratic Party Whip

'90   World Wide Web and first web page

'91   Internet becomes available to public

'92   Bill Clinton elected president

'94   Mandela elected president South Africa

'95   Bomb destroys Oklahoma City Federal Building, killing 168

      Toy Story first computer-generated movie

'96   Dolly the sheep, first cloned animal

'97   U.S. lands Pathfinder on Mars

      Harry Potter and the Philosopher's Stone published in the U.S.

'98   Google founded

      iMac marketed

'99   11 countries use Euro as currency

      Columbine High School shooting

'00 Supreme Court gives tight election to George W. Bush

'01 9/11 attack in New York and Washington

'02 Taliban (terrorist group) overthrown in Afghanistan

Department of Homeland Security created

'03 U.S. invades Iraq

Human Genome Project finished

Latinos now largest U.S. minority

U.S. captures Saddam Hussein of Iraq

'04 Facebook begins at Harvard

'05 Hurricane Katrina floods most of New Orleans and kills 1,600

'06 Hamas, an Islamist organization, wins Palestinian elections

'07 iPhone introduced

U.S. economy in crisis

'09 Barack Obama becomes first black president

INTRODUCTION

YOUNG HARRY REMOVED THE RIFLE from a peg near the door and checked the barrel. The seven chambers were empty and no one in town sold bullets. So he yanked open wooden drawers to look for some. He found two 22-caliber bullets and headed out.

He searched for a jackrabbit. At first, none crossed Harry's path. Was he wasting his time? Would his grandmother be disappointed?

Harry wandered along a dry creek bed. Behind him, a brilliant yellow-orange Nevada sun set in a cloudless blue sky. He had to find a jackrabbit while there was enough light. Then he spotted one. A two-foot-long, brown, furry animal with black-tipped ears rested just in front of him. It seemed to be daring Harry to shoot it.

Harry pulled the trigger. He missed. His prey didn't budge, still an easy target for the inexperienced hunter. Again, Harry raised the rifle, aimed, and shot. This time it sprinted away. Harry followed the blood trail of the injured animal. As his prey slowed, Harry caught and dragged it to his grandmother's house. The jackrabbit was dead before he reached the house. To prepare the animal for the large stew pot, he first skinned it. Next, he removed its head and organs. Then, his grandmother took over.

Because his grandmother didn't have anything for dinner, she had asked Harry to hunt for a rabbit. Ten-year-old Harry had provided and readied the necessary ingredient for her tasty jackrabbit stew. Many times the family wasn't lucky enough to have any meat. Sometimes they had no supper at all.[i]

COMING FROM SUCH a background of poverty, Harry Reid was unlikely to achieve success. Yet, he has been the majority leader of the United States Senate. President Obama counts on him to pass important legislation.

Today, Reid lives what people call "The American Dream."

His childhood, though, provided a formula for failure. Harry has said, "[N]o child should be raised the way I was raised."[ii]

He was a poor boy from a small town. The town didn't have a high school and offered few opportunities.

How did he become wealthy? How did he become Senate majority leader? How did he become one of most powerful men in Washington?

 The American Dream is hard to define. Some people think it means to be rich. Some feel owning a home is the dream. Others feel that having a better life than one's parents fulfills the dream. Some think that not living from paycheck to paycheck is the dream. How would you define it? Ask a parent how he or she would define it.

What is your dream? How likely are you to achieve it? What would you need to do?

As you read about Harry, see if you can figure out how he was able to achieve what he has.

---

[i] Harry Reid, *The Good Fight: Hard Lessons From Searchlight to Washington* (New York: Berkley Books, 2008), 47.
[ii] Ibid., 29.

PART 1

BEGINNINGS

SEARCHLIGHT

WHERE FEW WANT TO LIVE

HARRY WAS BORN IN THE SMALL TOWN of Searchlight, Nevada. It wasn't always small. For a brief time, the town flourished. That was shortly after the town was established in 1897. Before the 1890s, almost no one inhabited the area. Not even Native Americans wanted to live in the harsh environment.

Searchlight is located in the 25,000-square-mile Mohave Desert. The Mohave is larger than the combined size of Rhode Island, Delaware, Connecticut, Hawaii, and New Jersey. A desert receives less than ten inches of yearly precipitation. Searchlight's annual total is less than eight inches. The sun shines there 310 days a year. In such a climate, growing food is difficult because water resources are scarce.

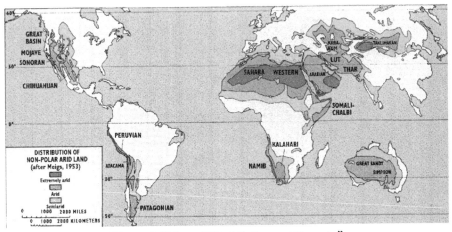

Figure 1: "Map of World's Largest Deserts."

Those who moved to the area had to be careful of the desert plants and animals. Anyone, especially children running about, might brush against the needle-like spines of the cholla cactus. A child could collide with the razor-sharp leaves of yucca plants or become entangled in grease brush or mesquite. A child wouldn't likely know that the Joshua trees, referred to by the National Park Service as "twisted, spiky trees straight out of a Dr. Seuss book," grow only in the Mohave.[iii]

Curious children might stop to watch mice, rats, jackrabbits, foxes, coyotes, scorpions, and Gila monsters scampering about. They would need to be alert for three- to six-foot-long, venomous Western Diamondback rattlesnakes or Mojave green rattlesnakes. Rattlesnakes of these types bite hundreds of people a year, and some of these bites can be deadly. Children and adults would also need to watch for scorpions and tarantulas.

Figure 2: Searchlight, Nevada

[iii] Jane Rodgers, "Joshua Trees," July 14, 2010, *National Park Service*, http://www.nps.gov/jotr/learn/nature/jtrees.htm.

Gold was discovered in 1894, and people poured into the area. In the hope of becoming rich, people endured the harsh surroundings. When miners began digging for the precious ore, water was discovered. One problem was solved. At the height of the boom, about 3,000 people lived in Searchlight. Nevada's entire population was little more than 42,000 at the time.

 In 1894, what percentage of the state's population lived in Searchlight? Reno existed, but it was small. Las Vegas wasn't established until 1905. So where did most of the population live? (Hint: Why did people pour into Searchlight? What other places in Nevada are known for mining?)

Where would you look to find the current populations of Reno, Las Vegas, and Henderson?

Miners needed services and supplies. For a brief time around 1906, during the gold rush, doctors, a dentist, and lawyers lived in town. Searchlight had a railroad, electricity, telephones, a telegraph office, and three stagecoach lines. The town had a hospital, a church, a school, feed stores, a meat market, and a bakery. It had rooming houses, nine saloons, and gambling halls. Searchlight, unlike many towns, had a tent factory, a watchmaker, a cigar manufacturer, and a bowling alley.[iv] The once-desolate area prospered. It had luxuries found in the larger cities of the East, such as Philadelphia, New York, or Boston. People could find anything they needed in Searchlight—that is, until the boom ended. When the gold gave out, people moved on. With fewer people, fewer supplies and services were needed.

[iv] Harry Reid, *Searchlight: The Camp That Didn't Fail* (Reno: University of Nevada Press, 1998), 54-55.

Harry Reid's grandfather was one of the men who came in search of wealth. His son, who was later known as Harry, Sr., became a miner and was one of the few who stayed. Even after the boom ended, Harry, Sr., worked the mines. A poor living could still be made from them.

A HARD LIFE IN A SMALL TOWN

HARRY REID, JR., was born on December 2, 1939, to Inez and Harry Reid, Sr. The ten-pound Harry[v] was delivered in his grandmother's two-room shack.[vi] His parents had two older children: Don, who was 12, and Dale, who was 10. Another brother, Larry, came along two years after Harry.

By the time Harry, Jr., was born, Searchlight had only 200 residents. Gone were the railroad, the hospital, and the church. Doctors, dentists, and lawyers went elsewhere. The doctor who delivered Harry left in early 1940.

The Reids didn't care that certain services were unavailable. Even in an emergency, the family couldn't afford a doctor, and they certainly couldn't pay a dentist.

Harry, Sr., served as his own dentist. He had no choice. He had no medicine with which to dull the pain. He had no dental tools with which to yank out his rotten teeth. Instead, he used his pliers and endured the pain.[vii] The young Harry squirmed as he watched his father pull out his own teeth.

---

[v] Reid, *The Good Fight*, 33.
[vi] Ibid., 24.
[vii] Ibid., 46.

His mother, too, had terrible teeth. Most fell out. She ate the soft foods a baby would eat. Harry was determined that one day he would pay for her dental treatment.[viii]

As Harry realized, the poor do what they can just to live day by day. Those who struggle to get by have a difficult time thinking or planning for a future.

 Think about it! When money is tight in your family, what don't you buy? Do you go without seeing a doctor or a dentist? Do you go without another pair of shoes? A toy? Dessert? Is your family unable to take a vacation? Go to the movies? How hard is it on you to go without these things?

Even though you are still a student, what could you do to help others who are less fortunate than you?

By Harry's tenth birthday, Searchlight had neither a grocery store nor telephone service. Cell phones hadn't been invented yet. Neither had television, microwaves, nor computers. When the El Rey Motel needed supplies, the owner sent messages by carrier pigeon.[ix] The kids surely enjoyed watching the pigeons take off and return.

Searchlight is in the southern part of Nevada, far from other places. Not until 1963 was there a paved road to Searchlight. Travel on unpaved roads is slow. A place 60 miles away might take more than three hours to reach. Laughlin, the closest town, is 39 miles to the southeast; Henderson is 40 miles northeast; and Las Vegas is 55 miles to the north. California's border is 20 miles west and Arizona's is 14 miles east. Travel to any of these places would take well over an hour. Even today, the nearest supermarket to Searchlight is 40 miles away.

[viii] Ibid., 46-7.

[ix] "El Rey-2012," *Queho Posse*, accessed July 26, 2015, http://www.quehoposse.org/index.php/plaques/43-el-rey.

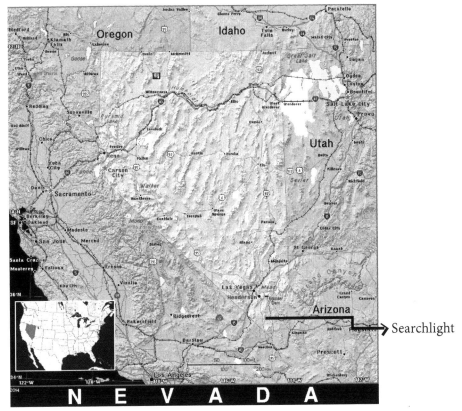

Figure 3: Map of Nevada (with Searchlight)

Not only was Searchlight remote when Harry was growing up, but it was also poor. It was a place where few opportunities were available.

In Searchlight, public school ended after eighth grade. For most students today, that's the end of middle school. A few attended high school in other towns.

When Harry began school, Searchlight had enough students to fill two classrooms. One teacher taught grades one through four. Another taught the fifth through eighth grades. Harry couldn't wait to attend school with the older students. By the time Harry reached fifth grade, few school-aged students lived in town. The school needed only one room.[x] He was disappointed that the older students had to remain with the younger ones.

---

[x] Reid, *The Good Fight*, 43.

How different would a one-room schoolhouse be from your school? How do you think a teacher handles so many different grades in one room? Would you like to attend a one-room schoolhouse?

Do you have friends who have been home-schooled? What is it like for them?

Figure 4: Elementary school Reid attended, now a recreation center.

Figure 5: The current Reid Elementary School in Searchlight, Nevada.

As a child, Harry lived with his parents, Harry, Sr., and Inez, and his brother Larry in a two-bedroom house. Necessity caused the Reids to recycle. Their house was made from railroad ties, which are logs used as the base of railroad tracks. Used railroad ties were a sign of poverty. His father covered the logs with chicken wire and plaster.[xi] Their house had a rough, stucco-like exterior. In recent years, a student who was looking at a picture of Reid's boyhood home thought it was a painting of Abraham Lincoln's log cabin.[xii]

Figure 6: The home where Harry Reid grew up.

The family had neither a toilet nor hot water. They used an outhouse. Larry, as the youngest, was lucky. He used a five-gallon bucket located in the room that he and Harry shared. Harry envied Larry for this "luxury." On winter nights, Harry's feet crossed the cold linoleum to the door leading outside.[xiii] Going out, not knowing what animal might lurk close by, was scary.

Hanging from the ceiling of the living room was a wooden star.[xiv] On one wall hung a pillowcase embroidered with President Franklin D. Roosevelt's words, "We can, we will, we must."[xv] In part because of these decorations, Harry felt he had a nice house.

The Reids had electricity and some electrical appliances. Since the electricity worked only sometimes, they needed both an electric stove and

[xi] Ibid., 26.
[xii] Unnamed Reid staffer, interview with author, December 5, 2012.
[xiii] Reid, *The Good Fight*, 26-7.
[xiv] Ibid., 26.
[xv] Ibid., 24.

a wood-burning one as backup. One of Harry's chores was to chop wood for the fireplace.

When the electricity worked, Harry, Jr., and his brother, Larry, enjoyed listening to the radio. It was one of the few luxuries Harry's family had. At the time, across the country, families often gathered around in the evenings to listen to music, comedy shows, mysteries, quiz shows, and baseball games.

 What was life like for your parents and grandparents? What items that you take for granted hadn't been invented? When did televisions become popular? Did television become a substitute for the family radio? Do computer games now substitute for TV? Did your grandparents have computers? How different would life have been without these? How does your family spend its evenings?

Harry's parents worked hard for the little money they earned. Though his father held a job, Harry, Sr., didn't have a steady income. Like many uneducated women, Inez Reid had few ways to earn money. However, she was fortunate enough to find work. She took in wash and ironed laundry from motels in town.

Typically, washday was tough. First, clothes were boiled. Then, they were tossed into a second tub to be rinsed in cold water. People used a ridged scrubbing board to loosen dirt. The wash would be wrung by hand and hung out to dry. Afterward, items would be ironed. The heavy irons were heated on wood stoves. At the end of an especially hot day, someone like Harry's mom was exhausted. People who could afford it started purchasing washing machines in the late 1940s.

Inez didn't give up, a trait Harry inherited from her. His hunt for the jackrabbit shows his perseverance.

The work Harry's mom did was tiring; however, the work Harry's father did was difficult and dangerous. He was a hard-rock miner. Underground mining used dynamite. After the blasts, the miners used shovels and picks to break away gold and minerals from the fallen rocks. Many miners died or were badly injured by the blasts.

Days before Harry, Jr., was born, his father was almost killed in a mining accident. On the near-fatal day, Harry, Sr., and his partner set the dynamite and lit the fuses. As his partner started his steep climb up the ladder, someone accidentally set off one of the blasts. Harry's father hadn't yet begun his ascent. His partner re-entered the mine and dragged the unconscious Reid to the surface. Just as they emerged from the shaft, the other blasts went off. The doctor estimated that 300 rock splinters were in Harry, Sr.'s left thigh and leg.[xvi]

Young Harry watched his mother dig out small rocks from his father's back.[xvii] What a terrible sight for a child to watch. At least Harry, Sr., whose brother had been killed in a similar accident,[xviii] had survived and been able to see his children grow up.

Workers knew hard-rock mining was both unsafe and exhausting.

Harry's father liked to work alone in the mines. Laws should have prevented Harry's father from doing so. However, no one enforced the laws. Harry's dad didn't complain since he enjoyed being alone.[xix]

Although Harry's father worked hard, he wasn't always paid. The mine owners sometimes kept his wages. Miners could do nothing about it. If they complained, they could be fired. When Harry's father wasn't paid, the family had no income except the small amount of money the laundry brought in. Harry and the other children disliked the owners for withholding the workers' pay. Harry knew his father deserved his earnings.

[xvi] Ibid., 34-35.
[xvii] Ibid., 33-35.
[xviii] Ibid., 35.
[xix] Ibid., 38.

FIGHTING AT HOME AND BEYOND

MINERS OFTEN SUFFERED from loneliness and breathing disorders. Some miners drank heavily, hoping alcohol would make them feel better.

Harry's father was one of those men. Harry's mother drank, too. People's behaviors can change when they drink too much. Nice people can sometimes show their mean sides. Drinking did this to Harry's father. Sometimes Harry, Sr., was drunk. Sometimes he hit his wife. Today, we call this type of behavior "domestic violence." It is against the law. For years, Harry listened to the beatings. He wanted them to stop. As a young boy, he couldn't do anything to stop his large, powerful father.

Domestic Violence

Domestic violence (DV) is a pattern of behavior in which violence, or the threat of violence, is used. It is called domestic violence when it occurs between people who are living together, whether they are married or not.[xx] The U.S. Department of Justice reported in September 2014 that about 25 percent of women had experienced DV during their lifetimes. About one million cases occur each year. Of these, 85 percent are against women, and 15 percent are against men. No one race, religion, economic group, or educational or cultural group is exempt from experiencing this violence. Each year, more than six million children in the U.S.

[xx] "Definition," last modified January 5, 2015, *Domestic Violence Handbook*, http://www.domesticviolence.org/definition.

witness domestic violence.[xxi] Children can talk to family members, teachers, counselors, or religious leaders to deal with what they see.

Harry also started fights. Children may imitate what they see at home. They may even continue the behavior in their own homes one day. Young Harry often didn't need a reason to fight. Once he fought a new kid in town: "…I was jealous of him. He probably dressed decently, was well-spoken. He was just different. The typical things that threaten people,"[xxii] Harry writes in *The Good Fight*, his autobiography. That fight ended in a draw.

Another time, he beat up his teacher's son. The teacher, Harry believed, favored her own son, and Harry felt the boy took advantage by bullying other students. Harry and some of the students disliked the boy's attitude. One day, Harry couldn't stand the boy's behavior anymore. So he took action in the only way he knew: He started a fight. As Harry later wrote, "So right there in the classroom, I beat the crap out of the kid, in front of all the other students and his own mother. I did such a good job beating him up that I broke my hand on his hard head."[xxiii]

Harry's father didn't punish him. In fact, he gave his son boxing lessons. Harry, Sr., explained the importance of closing a fist as a punch was delivered.[xxiv] Young Harry learned how to effectively deliver a punch. And he continued to get into fights.

In spite of picking fights with others, Harry hated seeing his father beat up his mother. One day after Harry, Sr., had beaten up Inez, 14-year-old Harry and 12-year-old Larry pinned their father to the floor.

[xxi] U.S. Department of Justice, Bureau of Justice Statistics, "Domestic Violence/Abuse Statistics," *Statistic Brain Research Institute*, last modified September 5, 2014, http://www.statisticbrain.com/domestic-violence-abuse-stats.
[xxii] Reid, *The Good Fight*, 41.
[xxiii] Ibid., 42.
[xxiv] Ibid., 42.

According to Harry's book, they didn't punch him or hit him. They just kept him pinned to the floor. Harry, Sr., yelled, kicked, and hit the boys for about 15 minutes. Then he relaxed and began to laugh. The match was over. Harry's father realized his sons were stronger than he, and the boys knew their mother was safe from further beatings. Since Harry's father respected physical strength, he didn't punish his sons.[xxv] Eventually, Harry learned that people respect other types of strength more.

What could you do if someone you knew were being beaten up at home? Would you talk to a teacher or school counselor about what you knew? Is there someone else you could talk to?

Do you join a group watching a fight and cheering on the fighters? Have you ever felt the urge to hit someone? How did you handle your feelings of anger?

At home, the fights stopped, but the drinking continued. Sometimes, the elder Reid was too drunk to work. Other times, he waited until after work to begin drinking. Harry's dad once became involved in a fight at a local bar. When he left the bar, he was arrested. The police beat Harry, Sr., and hauled him off to jail in Las Vegas. Several times, Harry's dad was sent to jail for disorderly conduct.[xxvi] Normally, Harry, Sr., wasn't a trouble-maker, but drinking affected his behavior.

One time, the sheriff took Harry, Jr., and some other youngsters for a short ride. On the road they stopped to look at an overturned car. The driver had been killed in the accident. The sheriff told them the driver had been driving drunk. The sheriff wanted to make an impression on the kids.[xxvii]

[xxv] Ibid., 52-53.
[xxvi] Ibid., 28-29.
[xxvii] Dick Polman, "Philadelphia Interview with Harry Reid about *The Good Fight: Hard Lessons from Searchlight to Washington*," Free Library, last modified May 9, 2008, http://libwww.freelibrary.org/authorevents/podcast.cfm?podcastID=94.

Harry may have realized that drinking problems can run in families. Now, as an adult, he doesn't drink at all.

FROM SEARCHLIGHT AND BACK AGAIN

T HE OLDER REID had many talents. He did carpentry, finishing work, and welding. He was also a blacksmith and worked on engines. All of those jobs paid better than mining. But Harry's tough, quiet, and independent father preferred life in the mines. At times, he undertook other work, but he loved mining and returned to it.

On at least two occasions, the elder Reid worked in Henderson, Nevada. Once was at the outbreak of World War II. Searchlight's mines had temporarily closed. Harry, Sr., took a job with Basic Magnesium in Henderson.[xxviii] Magnesium was used to make bombs. Those who worked at Basic Magnesium were excused from serving in the military. Their jobs were classified as "necessary to the war effort." The pay was on time, the hours were regular, and the chances of being hurt were minimal.

While Harry's father was at Basic Magnesium, his uncle Doug fought in Europe. Harry's uncle Jeff was stationed in the Pacific.[xxix]

World War II

World War II was the second time in the twentieth century that much of the world was at war. It raged from 1939 to 1945.

The German people felt the peace treaty after World War I had been too harsh. In the 1930s, Germany's economy was

---

[xxviii] Reid, *The Good Fight*, 36-37.
[xxix] Ibid., 43.

struggling, and its leaders wanted more land. Hitler became Germany's leader in 1934. He campaigned to expand Germany's borders. At first, their forces were successful in conquering other lands. They took over Austria, the Sudetenland, and Czechoslovakia.

No nation tried to stop Hitler until he ordered the German army to invade Poland in 1939. At that point, several nations realized that Hitler and Germany had to be stopped. Joining together as the Allied Powers, these nations declared war on Germany. Eventually, the Allied Powers included Great Britain, France, China, the Soviet Union, Canada, Australia, Belgium, Brazil, and the United States.

Joining Germany were Austria, Italy, and Japan, which became known as the Axis Powers.

After invading Poland, German forces attacked Denmark, Norway, the Netherlands, Belgium, Luxembourg, France, Greece, and other countries. Russia entered the war after the Germans invaded it in 1941. At first the Germans dominated. Eventually, the large territory and cold winters in Russia helped end Germany's push east.

Another part of Hitler's plan was to eliminate Jews and others who were viewed as "different." He and his followers, the Nazis, set up concentration camps where millions were killed. The dead included six million Jews. The death of so many Jews became known as The Holocaust.

Another five million non-Jews were killed. They included Gypsies, people with disabilities, the legally insane, Communists, Jehovah's Witnesses, homosexuals, and anyone who spoke out against the Nazis.

The United States didn't enter the war until the Japanese bombed Pearl Harbor in Hawaii on December 7, 1941. The United States became involved in the war in both Europe and Asia.

The Allied invasion of Europe began on the beaches of Normandy, in northern France. July 6, 1944, known as D-Day, marked the beginning of the attempt by the Allies to free Europe from German control. V-E Day was the day that victory in Europe was declared, in May of 1945.

The war continued in the Pacific. Some of the important battles in the Pacific were at Guadalcanal, Iwo Jima, Okinawa, and Midway.

A new and terrible weapon, the atomic bomb, was dropped on Hiroshima, Japan, on August 6, 1945. The Japanese didn't surrender. A second atomic bomb was dropped on Nagasaki seven days later.

The Japanese surrendered on September 2, 1945. The war had ended. Now the world needed to rebuild.[xxx]

Figure 7: "Wounded soldiers in a trench."

Figure 8: "U.S. soldiers take cover under fire somewhere in Germany."

[xxx] "World War II," *The Concise Columbia Encyclopedia, Second Edition* (New York, Columbia University Press, 1989). 907-8.

Figure 9: "U.S. Marines operating an M1919 A4 during World War II."

Figure 10: "Warsaw Ghetto Uprising."

Figure 11: "Coutances, France: one of many destroyed towns."

Figure 12: "Mushroom cloud from the atomic explosion over Nagasaki at 11:02 a.m., August 9, 1945."

Figure 13: "Nagasaki, Japan following the atomic bombing on August 9, 1945."

When four-year-old Harry moved to Henderson, he followed his older brothers around. Don and Dale attended Basic High School at the time. One day, Don allowed Harry to accompany him to basketball practice. Little Harry had strict instructions. He was not to speak to anyone nor get in anyone's way. The young boy obeyed his brother so well, Don forgot about him. Only when he reached home did Don remember he had left his brother behind at the school gym. He ran back to find Harry. Because Don didn't want trouble, he swore Harry to silence. Harry kept his word.[xxxi]

[xxxi] Reid, *The Good Fight*, 37.

Have you wanted to be with an older brother or sister? Did he or she want you following along? How did you handle the situation? If you are the older brother or sister, do your siblings want to be with you? How does it make you feel? How have you handled this situation? If your parents have taken sides, how have you felt about the decision?

Harry had relatives in Henderson. His Uncle Joe and Aunt Ray were related to him on his father's side. Joe was quiet, just like Harry, Sr., and Aunt Ray was religious. Also, young Harry's Aunt Jane owned a small restaurant and made delicious meals. When Harry attended high school in Henderson, he became close to his relatives there.[xxxii]

Figure 14: Harry Reid, Sr. (age 2) in 1916 with family. Front (L-R): Joe Reid; Harry Reid, Sr.; Jeff Reid, Jane Reid. Middle (L-R): Mason Reid, John Reid, Harriet Reid, Robert Reid. Back (L-R): John's mother, Ellen Misener.

Once the mines reopened, Harry, Sr., headed back to Searchlight and the mines. The family again struggled to earn a living.

Life in Searchlight was unexciting. For fun, Harry sometimes sat on a ridge and counted the cars heading to Las Vegas. It was something to do in a town that offered few activities.

[xxxii] Ibid., 106.

When he was 11, Harry began to accompany his father into the mines. He wore a helmet with a light attached. At first, Harry only supplied his father with companionship. As he became older and stronger, Harry helped shovel ore into carts. A day in the mines would leave them with scratched and bleeding knuckles and torn clothing. Both returned home dirty and tired. Harry didn't complain.[xxxiii]

As Harry became stronger, he earned money by his own hard labor. He shoveled dirt, carried water, and cleaned horse stalls. Although the dirt and smells in the stalls were sickening, it was an honest way to make money. One time, he dug trenches and postholes for a cowboy. Another time, some men who were drilling a well had thirteen-year-old Harry drive the water truck.[xxxiv]

Harry and his father sometimes dug graves. The land was so hard that the elder Reid used dynamite. This too was dangerous, but the family needed the extra money.

Harry didn't always get to keep his earnings. Sometimes Harry, Sr., took his son's hard-earned money. Unfortunately, it often went for alcohol.[xxxv]

Miners' sons often became miners as well. It's the only life they knew. Harry wanted something different. His brother Don had joined the United States Marines after completing high school. Don's steady and decent income might have tempted Harry. However, Harry chose a different path. Instead, like many kids, he dreamed of being an athlete. He loved baseball. Today, the soft-spoken Reid is thin and doesn't look athletic. Some people are surprised to learn that, as a youth, he played baseball and football, and fought in the ring.

[xxxiii] Ibid., 38-39.
[xxxiv] Ibid., 48-49.
[xxxv] Ibid., 233.

ALMOST ARRESTED

FORTUNATELY, WILLIE MARTELLO, the owner of the El Rey Motel in Searchlight, was a kind man. Otherwise, Harry might have found himself in jail.

Once a week during the summer, Martello allowed the neighborhood children to swim in, as Reid writes, the "fancy in-ground tiled pool" at the El Rey.[xxxvi] Splashing around in the cool blue water of the pool was a treat in 100-degree weather.

At Christmas, Martello gave each kid in Searchlight a five-dollar bill. Harry and the other children were thrilled. For many, including Harry, it was the largest bill they had ever held.[xxxvii]

In spite of Martello's kindness, Harry stole from him.

One day, Harry noticed cases of empty bottles stacked outside the motel. He and a high-school buddy took them. Both should have known better. Martello had planned to trade the bottles for money. Instead, it was Harry and his friend who traded them in. They thought they had gotten away with the crime and celebrated their good luck. But Martello had seen Harry take the cases. Later, he confronted the teen. He could have reported Harry to the police. As Reid writes in his autobiography,

---

[xxxvi] Ibid., 23.
[xxxvii] Ibid., 29.

Martello said, "I didn't get you in trouble, because I think you could amount to something. Don't you do stuff like that."[xxxviii]

At this point Harry seemed headed for trouble.

[xxxviii] Ibid., 55.

A DIFFERENT WORLD
OUTSIDE SEARCHLIGHT

HARRY LOVED LISTENING to baseball games on the radio. One afternoon, he was in Cleveland rooting for the Indians. Another, he was in New York listening to Yankees', Dodgers', or Giants' games. The Cleveland Indians was his favorite team. He disliked the Yankees because the team was usually the favorite. Harry preferred to root for the underdog.

He heard about Jackie Robinson's troubles as the first African-American in the major leagues. Until then, Harry had been unaware that, in parts of the country, blacks and whites didn't work together or go to the same schools. He was surprised to learn that blacks couldn't stay at the same hotels, eat in the same restaurants, or drink from the same water fountains as the white people did. He was unaware that blacks couldn't sit where they wanted on buses or in movie theaters.

The radio opened up the world for the young boy. Some of what he heard he disliked.

Jackie Robinson Integrates Baseball

Segregated baseball teams began in 1890. Blacks only played in the Negro leagues. Whites played in what was known as the Major Leagues (which included both the National and American Leagues). In 1947, change came. That year, Jackie Robinson was selected by the New York Dodgers to integrate the Majors.

Baseball's Major Leagues and the Negro League had begun playing segregated all-star games in 1933. Fans noticed the strong skills of African-American players during their all-star games. Also, exhibition games between the Negro League and Major Leagues demonstrated the skills of black players.[xxxix]

During World War II, African-Americans fought loyally and bravely for the United States. After fighting for freedom around the world, many African-Americans felt they should have equality at home. People thought it was time for a change. A place to start was with baseball.

Branch Rickey, the vice president of the then-New York Dodgers (now the Los Angeles Dodgers), took steps to make this happen. He evaluated men in the Negro League for the right combination of factors. He needed an outstanding athlete. But, just as importantly, he needed a man with the temperament and personality to handle difficulties. Rickey knew the first black player in the Majors would face prejudice.[xl]

Jackie Robinson seemed to be the right choice. At first, Robinson played on a farm team in Canada. There, he batted .349 and had a 98.5 percent fielding average.[xli] He was moved to the Dodgers.

Even Robinson's teammates wouldn't take the field with him, and they shouted nasty names. The Dodgers' manager, Leo Durocher, told his players he would prefer to trade them all rather than get rid of Robinson.[xlii]

Players from other teams refused to play the Dodgers because a black person was on the team.[xliii] In spite of threats and nasty comments, Robinson remained a gentleman.

[xxxix] "Negro League History 101," *Negro League Baseball*, P. Mills, publisher, accessed February 11, 2012, http://www.negroleaguebaseball.com/history101.html.
[xl] Gina DeAngelis, *Jackie Robinson* (Philadelphia: Chelsea House Publishers, 2001), 34-37.
[xli] "Jackie Robinson," Biography, *A&E Television Networks, LLC*, accessed February 12, 2012, http://www.biography.com/people/jackie-robinson-9460813#early-life.
[xlii] DeAngelis, *Jackie Robinson*, 48.
[xliii] Ibid., 52.

During his first year with the Dodgers, he hit twelve home runs, stole more bases than any other player in the National League, and helped the team win the National League pennant. He was so good that he received the Rookie of the Year Award.[xliv]

As Robinson continued to play great baseball, he gained many fans.

Later in the season, three more black players joined the Majors. By 1950, five teams were integrated, and by 1959, all teams fielded black players.[xlv]

It's hard to imagine a time when teams weren't integrated, or even to understand what Robinson faced.

Figure 15: "Jackie Robinson and Branch Rickey sign the contract that broke baseball's color barrier, August 28, 1945."

Figure 16: "Robinson in Dodgers uniform, 1954."

[xliv] "Jackie Robinson."
[xlv] DeAngelis, 57.

Figure 17: "Jackie Robinson sliding onto base."

Figure 18: "Congressional Gold Medal awarded to
Jackie Robinson."

Senator Reid still enjoys baseball. He can be seen at Washington, D.C. games rooting for the Washington Nationals.[xlvi]

When Harry was still a young man in Searchlight, Pop Paine, another Searchlight resident, was a retired Major League umpire. Payne talked to his neighbors about his job as an umpire. He had traveled the country and knew many of the players. Pop Payne's stories introduced young Harry to a world beyond Searchlight.

Harry's education was uneven. While he heard about life around the United States, he didn't receive any moral or religious teachings.

His parents hadn't taught him much about right and wrong. Neither had they taught him about honesty. However, his mother did provide him with one important lesson: He needed to have confidence in himself. She told him that he was as good as anyone else and could handle anything that came his way.[xlvii] With this advice and little more, Harry headed to high

[xlvi] Ivan V. Natividad, "Harry Reid Meets Up with New Nationals," *Roll Call*, May 4, 2012, http://www.rollcall.com/news/Harry-Reid-Meets-Up-With-New-Nationals-Outfielder-214273-1.html.
[xlvii] Reid, *The Good Fight*, 56.

school in Henderson—the same high school that his brothers, Don and Dale, had attended.

 What do you think of the lesson Inez Reid taught Harry? How important do you think values such as honesty or respect are? Is there something else you have been taught that is more important than what Harry learned? Is there something you think you should have been taught at home but weren't?

After he left for high school, Harry returned to Searchlight only for occasional visits. The town where he had been born was an embarrassment to him. In time, he would feel differently. He would realize that the small town where he had been born had affected whom he had become.[xlviii] In 1998, he wrote a book about Searchlight, a place that he had come to love: *Searchlight: The Camp That Didn't Fail.*

Only after he was elected to the United States Congress would he make Searchlight his home, but only part time. For most of the year, he needed to be in Washington, D.C., where he bought a one-bedroom condo at the Washington Ritz.[xlix] When in Nevada, he and his wife, Landra, would live part time in a double-wide trailer on property that he and his family owned in Searchlight. Around the year 2000, they built a two-bedroom, 3,000-square-foot home on the land. The Reids decorated their home with a mining theme, which included using a gate from one of Searchlight's mines. Next to it, by the entrance to the house, hung an abstract oil painting of Martin Luther King, Jr.[l]

[xlviii] Ibid., 54.

[xlix] Manu Raju, "Harry Reid: Ritz-Carlton Not Home," *Politico*, October 21, 2010, http://www.politico.com/news/stories/1010/43989.html.

[l] Elsa Walsh, "Minority Retort: How a Pro-Gun, Anti-Abortion Nevadan Leads the Senate's Democrats," *The New Yorker*, August 8, 2005, http://www.newyorker.com/magazine/2005/08/08/minority-retort.

On a visit to Searchlight with *New York Times* writer Adam Nagourney, Reid pointed out the Searchlight Cemetery, which dated from 1900. Reid told Nagourney, "I'm going to be buried here, and so is Landra."[li]

Then, in 2014, the Reids sold their property and several mining claims, which he had purchased over the years, for $1.7 million. He had bought a home in the Las Vegas area to be closer to his children and grandchildren.[lii]

But, back in 1953, as Harry was leaving Searchlight for high school in Henderson, he didn't know that Searchlight would never again be his full-time residence. He had no idea what the future held.

[li] Adam Nagourney, "Reid Battles in Washington and at Home," *The New York Times Magazine*, January 12, 2010, http://www.nytimes.com/2010/01/24/magazine/24reid-t.html.

[lii] Wesley Lowery, "Harry Reid Sells Searchlight Home, Will Move Closer to Family in Vegas," *The Washington Post*, June 9, 2014, http://www.washingtonpost.com/blogs/post-politics/wp/2014/06/09/harry-reid-sells-searchlight-home-will-move-closer-to-family-in-las-vegas/.

PART 2

MONEY STRUGGLES

HIGH SCHOOL AND BETTER TIMES

HOW WOULD HARRY REID, now a young teenager, deal with attending high school far from home? Where would he live? What new experiences would he have? Would he be happy?

High school provided Harry with the formal education his parents lacked. His mother had not completed high school, and his dad had only finished the eighth grade.[liii] However, both his parents loved to read, and they passed that love on to Harry. He still enjoys reading today. Even after he injured his right eye in 2015 and was unable to read, he listened to audiobooks.[liv]

Henderson, where he attended high school, was 40 minutes from Searchlight. Because of poor roads and transportation, traveling back and forth each day was difficult. On Mondays, Harry hitchhiked to Henderson. Hitchhiking was more common in the 1950s than it is today, especially in rural areas. Still, it was dangerous. He had to be careful.

Harry spent the school week in Henderson, where he stayed with relatives. On Fridays, he returned to Searchlight. This pattern continued for his first two years of high school.[lv] His parents moved back to Henderson

---

[liii] Harry Reid, *The Good Fight: Hard Lessons From Searchlight to Washington* (New York: Berkley Books, 2008), 27.

[liv] Steve Tetreault, "Reid Says He Expects Recovery After Eye Surgery," *Las Vegas Review-Journal*, January 22, 2015, http://www.reviewjournal.com/politics/reid-says-he-expects-recovery-after-eye-surgery.

[lv] Reid, *The Good Fight*, 106.

when Harry was a junior. Again, Searchlight had no work for Harry, Sr., but the magnesium plant had rehired him.[lvi]

Before he left for high school, Harry, Jr.'s nickname was "Pinky," "either for his pinkish skin tone or his reddish hair."[lvii] The name followed him to Basic High School. A high-school classmate of Harry's, Virginia Gutenberg, thought he had earned the name because his face turned red when he was embarrassed. She remembers him as polite, well-liked, and a good student.[lviii]

 Do you or someone you know have a nickname? Does the name come from the way the person is or from some form of his/her name? Explain.

In high school, Harry was busy.

As a freshman, he played football and baseball. He was left guard and defensive tackle on the football team. During both practices and games, Harry often ended up hurt. He ignored minor injuries and kept playing; just as he hadn't complained when he had broken his fist, he didn't complain about his football injuries, either. His coach admired Harry's spirit and told him so.[lix]

 Is complaining different from telling someone about a bad situation? Does it have to do with the topic, the tone of voice, or something else? If a person is seriously hurt, should he say something?

When would you complain about a situation? Is it when you've been hurt just a bit? A lot? When something is unfair?

[lvi] Ibid, 106.
[lvii] Erick Trickey, "Harry Reid," *Encyclopedia of World Biography*, accessed August 8, 2013, http://www.notablebiographies.com/newsmakers2/2006-Ra-Z/Reid-Harry.html.
[lviii] Virginia Gutenberg, telephone interview, March 3, 2015.
[lix] Reid, *The Good Fight*, 111.

> Do you know people who like to complain? If so, why do you think they do it?
>
> What do you think of kids who run to the teacher or to parents to tell what someone has done?

Harry was a catcher for the Basic High Wolves baseball team. In his sophomore year, the Wolves became both Nevada and California state champs. It was exciting and unusual to win two state championships. Because of its location near California, Basic High was permitted to play in a California league as well as a Nevada league. Harry became lifetime friends with Rey Martinez, who pitched for the Wolves' championship team. Many years later, Martinez would serve as Reid's chief of staff in the Senate.[lx]

In Searchlight, Harry had not attended church or been taught about religion. In high school, that changed. A football teammate invited Harry to attend "early morning school" at seven o'clock a.m. The well-liked Spanish teacher at Basic taught the class.[lxi]

His Aunt Ray encouraged him to attend. For the first time, Harry was taught religious beliefs. In particular, he learned about the Church of Jesus Christ of Latter-day Saints. It is also known as the LDS or Mormon Church. In his second year of high school, Harry lived with his Uncle Joe and Aunt Ray. His aunt was a Mormon. She was kind and took good care of him. Harry liked the Mormons he met. He learned that his mother's family had been Mormons at one time.

Mormon Church

The Church of Jesus Christ of the Latter-day Saints is the fourth-largest Christian denomination in the United States.[lxii] It has

---

[lx] Ibid., 111.
[lxi] Ibid., 108-109.
[lxii] "Largest U.S. Churches, 2012." *Infoplease*, accessed January 8, 2015, http://www.infoplease.com/world/religion/largest-us-churches.html.

over 6 million members in the United States, while worldwide statistics in 2012 show the church claims more than 15 million followers.[lxiii]

Joseph Smith founded Mormonism in 1830. Mormon head-quarters are in Salt Lake City, Utah.[lxiv]

Harry's schedule was already full as he entered his senior year, yet he decided to take on another activity. Why? Someone new to Basic High School had inspired him. This person taught history at the high school and boxing at a local center. Even as a child, Harry had liked to pick fights with kids he thought he could defeat. However, he hadn't thought about boxing until he saw Mike O'Callaghan in action. How thrilling it was to watch the wooden-legged O'Callaghan in the ring! Watching his history teacher, Harry realized he could, as he writes, "channel my brawling instincts into something more respectable."[lxv] Later, Harry learned that Mike O'Callaghan had lost his left leg in the Korean War. Some might have considered a missing limb a disability, but not O'Callaghan.

 Think about it! Do you know someone who has had to deal with a physical problem? What about someone who only had a broken wrist, arm, or leg? How did that person handle it? What do you know about the Special Olympics?

[lxiii] "Facts and Statistics," Newsroom, *Church of Jesus Christ of Latter-Day Saints*, last modified February 21, 2012, http://www.mormonnewsroom.org/facts-and-statistics/country/united-states/.

[lxiv] John Gordon Melton, "Mormon Religion, *Encyclopaedia Britannica*, accessed June 8, 2015, http://www.britannica.com/topic/Mormonism.

[lxv] Reid, *The Good Fight*, 42.

Korean Conflict

After World War II, Korea was split at the 38th parallel. North Korea had a communist government. Its regime was supported by China and Russia, two communist countries, while the United States occupied South Korea. The two Koreas were in conflict. In June 1950, North Korea invaded South Korea. President Truman called U.S. military forces to Korea. General MacArthur led them, along with those from fifteen other countries. These soldiers were members of a joint United Nations force.

The advantage shifted to South Korea. The communists realized they couldn't win, so they agreed to a peace treaty, which was signed in July 1953. By the time the fighting ended, 40,000 Americans had died and 100,000 had been wounded. Estimates place Chinese and Korean deaths at ten times those of the United States.

This fighting in the 1950s was called a "police action," not a war. To be called a war, the United States Congress must approve a Declaration of War. However, President Truman, for various reasons, chose not to ask Congress for the declaration.[lxvi]

Today, North and South Korea are separate countries. North Korea is a closed society ruled by a dictator. South Korea elects its president, much as we do here in the United States, and its citizens enjoy the freedoms of a democracy.

The two countries are still in conflict.

Figure 19: "The two Koreas, split at the 38th Parallel."

[lxvi] History Channel, "Korean War," *A&E Television Networks, LLC*, accessed January 8, 2015, http://www.history.com/topics/korean-war.

Figure 20: "United Nations' forces at the 38th Parallel, retreating back to the south from Pyongyang, in 1950."

Figure 21: "Pfc. Julias Van Den Stock of Company A, 32nd Regimental Combat Team, 7th Infantry Division, 1951."

Figure 22: "Men of the 1st Cavalry Division fighting in a train yard in Pyongyang, Korea."

Like many athletes, Harry and the other boxers built up their strength by running. O'Callaghan would ride behind the boys and threaten that if they were too slow, he would run them over.[lxvii] Of course, O'Callaghan was

---

[lxvii] Reid, *The Good Fight*, 114.

just joking. As an adult, Reid continued running. He entered twelve marathons, including the famous Boston Marathon held every year in April. An injury eventually put an end to his running.[lxviii]

Harry proved to be a good fighter. However, O'Callaghan only allowed Harry to spar: He could take part in practices but not in actual fights. Harry weighed enough to be a heavyweight, a category for grown men. O'Callaghan watched out for him. The young fighter could be badly injured against adults.[lxix] Until O'Callaghan's death, he remained an important part of Harry's life.

At Basic High School, Harry became interested in what would be his lifelong passion: politics. In his junior year, he ran in his first election, for the position of class treasurer. He was elected, and was surprised that people had actually voted for him.[lxx] His confidence grew. As a senior, friends encouraged him to run for student-body president. Only a senior could be elected to that position. Harry's opponent had been president of the freshman, sophomore, and junior classes. With Rey Martinez as his campaign manager, Harry ran against the three-time class president and won.[lxxi] Even Harry was surprised. Because of his win, he had added yet another activity to his schedule.

Perhaps because he was student-body president, he participated in a youth forum that dealt with issues of the day. He and Lorraine Hunt, who would one day become Nevada's lieutenant governor, were finalists. Each wrote an editorial for a column in the *Las Vegas Sun* called "Where I Stand."[lxxii] Because of his column, Harry's picture appeared on the front page of the newspaper on December 7, 1956.

[lxviii] Elsa Walsh, "Minority Retort: How a Pro-Gun, Anti-Abortion Nevadan Leads the Senate's Democrats," *The New Yorker*, August 8, 2005, http://www.newyorker.com/magazine/2005/08/08/minority-retort.

[lxix] Reid, *The Good Fight*, 114.

[lxx] Ibid., 112.

[lxxi] Ibid., 112-113.

[lxxii] Mark Adams, "The Forum That Foreshadows: Notable Alumni from the Sun Youth Forum," *Las Vegas Weekly*, November 13, 2013, http://www.lasvegasweekly.com/as-we-see-it/2013/nov/13/notable-alumni-sun-youth-forum/.

Think about it! What pastimes do you already have that might stay with you the rest of your life? Do you know others who have the same interests?

Do members of your family have interests that they developed as children? How difficult is it for them to continue with those activities as adults?

How likely are you to try something new? Why or why not? What do you think is worse, trying something and not succeeding or *not* trying and wondering whether you could have succeeded?

In addition to his school activities, Harry held a job at a doughnut shop. He had little choice in the hours. From four in the morning until school began, he dipped doughnuts in sugar glaze.[lxxiii] Not surprisingly, as an adult, Harry isn't too fond of glazed donuts, since he got so tired of them while working at this job!

Attending school and holding down a job was difficult. With his sports activities, student-government offices, and roles in school plays, Harry's day was long. He neither ate well nor slept enough, which weakened his body. Eventually, he became very sick. When Harry developed what might have been rheumatic fever, his girlfriend's family cared for him.[lxxiv] He was unable to attend school or work until he was well. In a way, his illness helped him to slow down.

Rheumatic Fever

Rheumatic fever begins with strep throat. Strep throat is caused by a bacteria called streptococcus. If the bacterial infection is treated at the beginning of the sore throat, it doesn't develop into

---

[lxxiii] Reid, *The Good Fight*, 112.
[lxxiv] Ibid., 113.

rheumatic fever. Since the mid-1940s penicillin has been used to treat strep throat.[lxxv] If left untreated, streptococcus may develop into rheumatic fever and cause permanent heart damage.[lxxvi]

Like many teenagers who work, Harry put most of his earnings into buying a car. It wasn't expensive or fancy, but it ran.

He also saved money so that he could pay for his mother's dental work. The first dentist he consulted looked at Harry's poor clothing and asked how he intended to pay. Harry, who had been taught he was as good as anyone else, disliked the dentist's attitude and walked out of his office. The second dentist Harry visited treated him respectfully.[lxxvii] Harry's earnings paid to repair his mother's teeth. He felt proud to help her. She no longer needed to eat the soft rice and potatoes she had lived on for years.

 Why does the way we look affect the way some people treat us? Is it fair? How important is it to express ourselves through our dress? If someone knows what is expected, why should or shouldn't that person follow the standard?

With his interest and skill in football and baseball, Harry planned to be a professional athlete. Athletics had made him popular, and athletics provided him with a college scholarship. But Harry was not destined for that life.

In his senior year, Dorothy Robinson, a counselor at Basic, spoke with Harry. Based upon his test scores, she suggested he study law. He was pleased that she cared enough to help him. Harry had no idea what a lawyer did, but, that day, Harry decided to become one.[lxxviii] He was becoming aware that he wasn't fast enough, large enough, nor good enough to earn a living as an athlete.

[lxxv] A. Saxena. "Rheumatic Fever and Long-term Sequelae in Children," *Current Treatment Options in Cardiovascular Medicine*, 4, no. 4(2002): 309-319, accessed April 21, 2015, http://www.ncbi.nlm.nih.gov/pubmed/12093388.

[lxxvi] "Diseases and Conditions Rheumatic Fever," *Mayo Clinic*, accessed April 21, 2015, http://www.mayoclinic.org/diseases-conditions/rheumatic-fever/basics/causes/con-20031399.

[lxxvii] Reid, *The Good Fight*, 46-47.

[lxxviii] Ibid., 115.

Though Harry was an average student,[lxxix] high school was good for Harry. To him, though, meeting Landra Gould was like winning a gold medal in an Olympic event. When he looked at Landra the first time, Harry thought she looked like a movie star. He described her as having "clear skin, dark hair and eyes, and a beautiful smile."[lxxx] They began to date in his third year at Basic; Landra, a sophomore, was a cheerleader.

She was the only child of Earl and Ruth Gould. Earl Gould, often called Doc Gould, worked in the medical field helping those with problems of the spine. The Goulds' new three-bedroom home looked like a palace to Harry.[lxxxi]

At first her family was kind to him. The Goulds cared for Harry throughout the course of his illness as though he were their child. Eventually, however, their kindness to Harry changed. His relationship with their daughter seemed to be getting serious. Landra dated Harry in spite of her parents' disapproval, and resentment grew between her parents and Harry. Harry left high school with a girlfriend, a career choice, and a scholarship to play football. The scholarship covered his tuition at the College of Southern Utah. In addition, O'Callaghan convinced a few businessmen to help Harry financially. They established a small scholarship for Harry.[lxxxii] The money helped with living expenses. However, Harry still needed to work.

It seems that much of Harry's future had been determined in high school. Life was looking good.

[lxxix] Suzan DiBella, "Connected at the Roots," *UNLV Magazine*, Fall 2004, accessed December 9, 2014, http://news.unlv.edu/unlvmagazineIssues/Fall04/reid.html.
[lxxx] Reid, *The Good Fight*, 99.
[lxxxi] Ibid., 100.
[lxxxii] Ibid., 118.

AND MORE SCHOOL

BAD LUCK, SUPPOSEDLY, comes in threes. And during his freshman year in Cedar City, it did.

After arriving at college, he received a sports injury early in football season. The injury caused nerve damage to his foot. He could no longer play college football.[lxxxiii] Instead of complaining about bad luck, he concentrated on his grades.

Next, his car broke down. He hadn't put in antifreeze. Having lived in the desert of Nevada, he wasn't accustomed to early freezes.[lxxxiv] September in Searchlight is still hot. In December, temperatures in Southern Nevada range from the 20s to the 50s. Cold weather came earlier to Cedar City. Within a week of arriving at school, temperatures fell below freezing. His car's engine froze. Harry had no money for repairs, nor to buy another car.[lxxxv]

Worst of all, Harry missed Landra. She was in Henderson finishing high school. He expected her to join him at the College of Southern Utah the following year. Then she received a full scholarship to attend the University of Nevada, Las Vegas (UNLV). The thought crossed Harry's mind that Dr. Gould might have encouraged some people to offer Landra a scholarship.[lxxxvi]

[lxxxiii] Ibid., 117 & 120.
[lxxxiv] Ibid., 118.
[lxxxv] Ibid., 118.
[lxxxvi] Ibid., 122.

Harry knew Landra should use the well-deserved opportunity to attend UNLV. Harry felt proud of her for earning the scholarship. In her freshman year, Harry would come back to Henderson to visit her, and he would show up at games to watch her cheer.[lxxxvii] As it turned out, though, Landra didn't graduate from college.

[lxxxvii] DiBella.

ANOTHER ROUTE?

WHEN ONE PATH closes, Harry usually finds another. Since he was unable to play college football, he took up boxing again. Over a two-year period, he took part in fifteen to twenty fights. He was paid to spar with professional fighters to help them train. Fights provided him with pocket money.[lxxxviii]

Think about it! Has there been a time when you faced a difficulty in which you had to rethink what you had been doing? How did it turn out? As you think back, is there something you could have done another way that might have led to better success?

Do you know whether either of your parents or another family member had to face a difficulty and rethink what he or she had been doing? If so, how did it turn out?

Boxing taught him skills that he would later adopt as a politician. He learned how to use an opponent's weaknesses against him. He learned when to fake a punch and when to avoid the opponent. He learned to wait for the right moment to attack an opponent. And he also came to realize that when "you have the opponent on the ropes, you finish him off."[lxxxix]

[lxxxviii] Reid, *The Good Fight*, 120.

[lxxxix] Paul Begala, "Harry Reid: King of the Hill," *CNN*, October 17, 2013, http://www.cnn.com/2013/10/17/opinion/begala-shutdown-showdown.

Harry also worked several jobs to survive. He pumped gas in the freezing cold. Until the 1970s, gas station attendants pumped gas for customers. At one point, he drove an oil truck.[xc] He worked at whatever odd jobs he could find.

Despite money hardships, Harry enjoyed college. He roomed with two friends from Basic High. The three teenagers acted immaturely, pulling various pranks. A fourth roommate, who had fought in Korea, ignored them.[xci] Though Harry enjoyed himself, he also earned good grades. He was elected freshman-class president.[xcii] He became involved in national politics when he organized a Young Democrats chapter on the college campus.[xciii]

 Think about it! How would you define a prank? Do you or your friends pull pranks on others? Do you have one you especially like to do? Do you have fun pulling a prank? How do others feel about them?

Cedar City, surrounded by mountains, is a lovely city, just north of the Mohave Desert, with pine, fir, and cedar trees. Harry liked this change of scenery. His heart, though, was in Henderson, and he stayed in contact with Landra.

[xc] Reid, *The Good Fight*, 118.
[xci] Ibid., 119.
[xcii] Ibid., 117.
[xciii] Ibid., 134.

AN ELOPEMENT

T HE GOULDS WERE unhappy with the relationship between Landra and Harry. They seemed opposed to it for only one reason: Harry wasn't Jewish. Landra had been raised as an observant Jew, and her parents wanted her to marry someone of the same religion. Harry felt religion shouldn't stand in the way of love. Her parents felt otherwise.[xciv]

Judaism

Judaism is the oldest of the world's religions that believe in one God. It is about 3,500 years old. The Jewish Sabbath, or day of religious observance, begins at sundown on Friday. It ends at sundown on Saturday. An observant Jew follows rules about eating and following the Sabbath that are different from those of Christians.[xcv]

Earl Gould had thought Landra and Harry would break up when Harry left for college, but they hadn't. Harry had sent Landra lots of letters during her senior year. Returning to Henderson during the summer of 1958, Harry continued to date her.

Dr. Gould decided that the time had come to end the relationship. One evening, her father refused to let Landra out of the house. According

---

[xciv] Ibid., 117.
[xcv] Myrtle Langley, "The Jewish Nation," *Eyewitness Religion* (London: DK Publishing, 2012), 46-51.

to Harry, Dr. Gould met him at the door and told him to leave. Harry refused. Their voices became louder, and the doctor shoved his daughter's date. Harry countered with a punch. In an instant, they were fighting in the front yard. The two figures were unevenly matched. Harry was heavier and taller, and he knew how to box, so he had the advantage. As the fight wound down, Harry found Landra at his side.[xcvi]

Landra risked her parents' anger to be with Harry. The couple eloped in September 1959. A Mormon bishop whom they knew performed the ceremony; he saved the newlyweds $25 by not charging to perform the ceremony.[xcvii]

Neither Harry nor Landra wanted a permanent split with her parents. Just after the wedding, Landra called them and told them she had married Harry. Her parents weren't happy. However, they told Landra that they loved her and wanted her happiness. Landra stayed in touch with her parents. In time, the Goulds accepted Harry as part of the family. The Reids kept a mezuzah, a Jewish symbol, on the doorpost of their Searchlight home.[xcviii] While Landra's parents were alive, the family celebrated both Jewish and Mormon traditions. Harry wanted his children to know about their mother's heritage.

Years later, when Dr. Gould died, Harry received the ring the doctor had always worn. By passing his ring on to his son-in-law, Dr. Gould showed his love and acceptance of Harry.

[xcvi] Ibid., 122-123.

[xcvii] Ibid., 124.

[xcviii] Adam Nagourney, "Reid Battles in Washington and at Home," *The New York Times Magazine*, January 12, 2010, http://www.nytimes.com/2010/01/24/magazine/24reid-t.html.

LIFE AS A MARRIED MAN

THE COUPLE HEADED to Logan, Utah, after their elopement. There, Harry had an academic scholarship to study history and political science at Utah State. Academic scholarships are awarded to students who have done well in school.

One hundred years earlier, Mormons had founded Logan, and more than 90 percent of the students at Utah State were Mormon. The family who allowed the Reids to rent space from them were LDS members. They were kind and generous to the young couple. While living with and observing this family, Harry learned more about the Church of Jesus Christ of Latter-day Saints. He liked what he learned.

Landra also liked what she was learning about the LDS church. Her 90-minute commute to work gave her a chance to chat with the Mormon bus driver. She invited him to the Reids' home so that she and Harry could learn more about the church. Since the teachings fit their ideas about how they wanted to live, they officially joined the Mormon Church.[c]

Eventually, Harry would hold several church offices, including being an elders quorum president and Sunday-school superintendent. For a while, he visited several LDS families each month to make sure they were doing well.[ci]

---

[c] Reid, *The Good Fight*, 127-128.

[ci] Christopher Smith, "Senate's New Majority Whip: Senator Harry Reid of Nevada," *Salt Lake Tribune*, June 9, 2001, http://www.adherents.com/largecom/lds_Reid.html.

Mike O'Callaghan had helped Harry in the past. In Logan, two faculty members at Utah State also took an interest in Harry. The first, Professor Leonard Arrington, was an economist and a Mormon scholar. Harry helped him grade papers. The other, Harmon Judd, a political-science professor, gave him some advice. As Harry wrote, Judd told him, "You obviously have a good mind, but your grammar is atrocious. You really should do something about it."[cii] Harry appreciated the advice, and enrolled in basic English classes. As a lawyer, he would need to come across as educated.

 How would you handle advice? Would it depend on who is offering it? Would it make a difference if it were a brother or sister, a parent, a teacher, or a stranger?

Has anyone offered advice that you've taken? How did it turn out? Has someone offered you advice that you ignored? How did that turn out?

While he was in his last year at Utah State, Landra gave birth to their first child. She could no longer work. In the early 1960s, few women with children were employed outside the home. Since day care wasn't common, women had little choice about whether to work; they needed to stay home to care for their children. So, after their daughter, Lana, was born in March 1961, Landra didn't earn any money. The couple struggled on Harry's small income. Fortunately, later that year, Harry received his degree.

Women and Work

Until the 1960s, in many places in the United States, women faced restrictions on what they could or couldn't do. Women couldn't borrow money, rent cars, buy houses, or have credit cards in their own names.

[cii] Reid, *The Good Fight*, 129.

Most women who did hold jobs were teachers, secretaries, typists, clerical workers, waitresses, nurses, librarians, salesgirls, servants, or cooks.

There were no female bus, cab, or truck drivers, news reporters, nor sportscasters.

A few brave, usually unmarried, women, entered fields in which men held the majority of the jobs. A few became doctors, scientists, or top-level business professionals. Women were paid lower salaries than men with the same jobs.

Equal pay for equal work was an idea that wasn't accepted.

Temporarily, during World War II, women held jobs that were traditionally done by men. But after the war ended, when men returned to the workforce, most women went back to the same types of jobs they had held before the war.

Until the 1960s, women tended to stay home. Several books about women's rights and their role in society encouraged them to work outside their homes. As they did so, opportunities opened up for women.

After Harry graduated from college, he needed a law degree to pursue his dream. Because he graduated in the top ten in his class at Utah State University,[ciii] Harry was likely to be admitted to any law school he chose. Nevada didn't have any law schools. So Harry turned to Mike O'Callaghan, still a teacher at Basic High, for advice. Mike convinced Harry to attend school in Washington, D.C. Many lawyers who practiced in Nevada had graduated from D.C.'s law schools. Nevada's first accredited law school didn't open until 1998.

[ciii] DiBella.

MONEY PROBLEMS AND MORE MONEY PROBLEMS

HARRY FOLLOWED O'CALLAGHAN'S advice. He and his family moved to Washington, D.C., and Harry was accepted into George Washington University, which he attended during the day. At night, he served as a policeman with the United States Capitol Police; O'Callaghan had helped him to get the job. The only time Harry could study was early in the morning, before class. He slept only a few hours each day, thanks to his school, work, and parenting duties. No doubt he was tired all the time. The last time he had worked long hours and gone to school, he had ended up with rheumatic fever. Although law school was difficult and time-consuming, Harry had no choice. He needed to earn a living for his young family, attend his classes, and study hard.

Then the Reids' car stopped. After tuition was paid, the young couple could hardly afford the basics in the expensive Washington, D.C. area. Certainly, no money was available for extras, including car repairs.

Another unplanned expense came along. They were expecting another a baby. Harry didn't know what to do. He decided to speak to the dean of the law school. Maybe some financial aid might be available. In general, financial aid was unavailable in the 1960s. Only those who could afford the cost attended college or graduate school. The dean suggested that Harry quit. Harry almost did.[civ]

[civ] Reid, *The Good Fight*, 133.

Landra refused to let him. She, no doubt, reminded him that he had spent years working hard for a law degree. He had just a little time left to finish up. Somehow, they would manage.

Figure 23: Harry Reid in law school.

Harry once again looked for a new path to accomplish a goal. Together, Landra and he formed a plan. Harry would take as many classes as he could. He would go to summer school in order to finish more quickly and return to Nevada.

The car was repaired, thanks to a local Mormon bishop, who provided them with a loan.[cv] It was this type of kindness from Mormons that had attracted the couple to the Mormon faith. As with all Harry's loans, this one too was repaid. Harry had transportation and a plan to finish. He felt optimistic.

[cv] Ibid., 133.

PART 3

AT LAST, THE WORKING WORLD

MAKING A NAME FOR HIMSELF

ARRY GRADUATED EARLY. Until he found full-time work as a lawyer, money would be a problem. A lawyer cannot practice in any state without a license in that state. To obtain one, he or she must pass a test called a Bar Exam. Each state sets its own date for the test.

In 1964, the Nevada Bar Exam was to be given in September, as it was each year in the 1960s. However, Harry would not be graduating in May, as most of his fellow law-school students were. In the states that gave exams in September, May graduates spent the long, hot summer studying. In the early 1960s, only half of those who took the test passed.

Bar Exam

The Bar Exam is a test people must take if they wish to practice law. Only Delaware and North Dakota still give the exam once a year because they don't have enough applicants to offer the test more often. Most states now offer the exam several times a year. Currently in Nevada, it is offered in July and February.

The test is given over a two-day period, and it contains both essay and multiple-choice questions about anything that has been covered in law school. Often the test requires specific knowledge of the laws in the state in which the exam is given.

> During the 2013-2014 congressional year, just under 40 percent of members of both branches of Congress were lawyers, but 55 percent of senators hold law degrees.[cvi]
>
> Six U.S. presidents have been law-school graduates: Barack Obama, Bill Clinton, Gerald Ford, Richard Nixon, William Taft, and Rutherford B. Hayes.[cvii] President Barack Obama even taught at the University of Chicago, Law School.[cviii]

Only those who have graduated from law school are allowed to take the Bar. If Harry wanted to take it early, he would need special permission.

So Harry faced a dilemma. Should he risk taking the exam before finishing law school? How much would his professors teach during the last semester? One semester accounted for one-sixth, or about 16 percent, of his law-school education. If he were to pass the exam, he could begin practicing as soon as he graduated. If he were to fail, he would once again need money for the exam, and he would have to wait to retake the test months after graduating.

Or should he wait to take the exam in September, after he graduated? He would have completed law school almost nine months earlier. In the meantime, he would be unable to work as a lawyer. However, extra months of study would likely increase his chance of passing the difficult and important exam. It was also possible that he could forget a lot if he delayed.

Harry made his decision. He would try to take the exam in September of 1963, before graduating. So he sent a formal request to the Nevada Supreme Court asking to be allowed to take the test early.[cix]

In order to take the exam, he would need money for a plane ticket to Nevada as well as for the exam fee. This fee was $50, which may not sound

---

[cvi] Jennifer Manning, "Membership of the 113th Congress: A Profile," *Congressional Research Service*, last modified November 24, 2014, http://fas.org/sgp/crs/misc/R42964.pdf.

[cvii] "Where Did All the American Presidents Go to College?," *Success Degrees*, accessed April 27, 2015, http://www.successdegrees.com/collegeeducationofamericanpresidents.html.

[cviii] "Media Inquiries," *The Law School, The University of Chicago*, accessed April 27, 2015, http://www.law.uchicago.edu/media.

[cix] Reid, *The Good Fight*, 155.

like a lot. However, in 1963, the value of fifty dollars would be the equivalent of $375 today. That was a large sum for someone who rarely had a spare dollar. Mike O'Callaghan, who was still teaching at Basic High, came to Harry's aid. He loaned Harry a $50 bill, the largest bill Harry had ever seen.[cx]

What Things Cost

What do you like to eat? See the chart below to find out what some of your favorite foods would have cost in the 1960s.[cxi] The prices seem low now, but people still complained about the high cost of food because they earned less money then.

Item	Food Costs in 1960s *Average Across the US*	Food Costs in 2013 *In Reno, Nevada (average from various supermarkets)*
Macaroni and Cheese	39 cents	$1.19
Fresh Corn	6 for 25 cents (4 cents an ear!)	5 for $1.00 (on sale)
Peanut Butter	79 cents	$3.49
Donuts	One dozen for 49 cents (4 cents a donut!)	About $5
Apples	3 pounds for 49 cents (that's 16 cents a pound)	$1.89/lb.

---

cx Ibid., 50.

cxi "1960's Food and Groceries Prices," *The People History,* accessed July 7, 2013, http://www.thepeoplehistory.com/60sfood.html.

Bananas	10 cents a pound	59 cents/lb.
Oranges	2 dozen for 89 cents (not quite 4 cents each)	$1.99/lb.
Fast Food Burger	20 cents	$1
Cheerios	28 cents a package	$3.79 for an 8.9-ounce package
Ice Cream	79 cents for half a gallon	$3.50 for a half gallon

To prepare for the exam, Harry did what many star athletes do. He studied hard and psyched himself up. He pictured himself taking the exam and doing well.

Because it takes weeks to receive the test results, most test-takers wait anxiously. Their futures depend on the results. Harry knew his chances of passing were slim, but he couldn't sit around worrying. He was still busy studying for his degree; he still had to complete school.

Finally, Harry learned that he had passed the exam. After graduation, he could practice law in Nevada. Now, he just needed a job.

This time, help came from his father-in-law. Dr. Gould convinced the City of Henderson to hire Harry as the city attorney. After all, Dr. Gould argued, Harry had graduated from high school in Henderson, and he was the only person in the town with a law degree.[cxii] His argument proved persuasive. Harry was offered the job.

As city attorney, he helped revise the city charter, the document that governs the city. By working to acquire federal lands, he increased Henderson's boundaries.

[cxii] Reid, *The Good Fight*, 156.

However, serving as city attorney was only a part-time position, so his pay was little. By joining a law firm in Las Vegas, Harry had an additional way to earn money. He needed clients—paying clients. At first, until he established his reputation, he had few.

Between his two jobs, Harry worked long hours. He had done that before. Slowly, he built his law practice.

In a little over twenty years, Harry tried more than one hundred cases before a jury.[cxiii] That's a large number for most lawyers.

He took all clients that came his way. A paying client was better than none. He represented robbers, drug addicts, and people filing for divorce. While going through a divorce, husbands and wives can be very angry at one another. Several clients in Nevada divorce cases had even killed their lawyers. To protect himself, Harry kept a loaded gun in his drawer. Even today, Harry believes in the people's right to carry weapons, a Second Amendment right.

He liked difficult cases. He liked cases others avoided. Often, these involved people who had little money and had been treated unfairly.

Our laws are written to protect citizens. Most people hire lawyers to help them obtain justice. Unfortunately, only people with money can afford lawyers. In 1974, Congress passed a law so that the poor could also have legal help.

What If Your Family Can't Afford a Lawyer?

Even someone with little or no income can obtain legal help. In 1974, the United States Congress created the Legal Services Corporation (LSC) to solve legal problems.

In Nevada, Nevada Legal Services provides this service. This organization assists people with problems relating to food stamps, unemployment benefits, or welfare. It helps with Medicaid

---

[cxiii] Ibid., 157

eligibility or with lost housing assistance. Its employees provide information about consumer and family law. For Native Americans, the service helps with various issues that affect this population directly, such as any cases in Tribal Courts, or with drawing up wills when tribal land is involved.[cxiv]

Some lawyers do *pro bono* work. They volunteer their time. Pro bono is a Latin term meaning "for the public good."

Some lawyers will work on a contingency basis. This means that they are paid only if they win a case in which money is involved.[cxv]

Harry took cases from people who had little money. He handled them on a contingency basis. If he won, he received a percentage of the money awarded to his client. If he lost, he received nothing. In this way, he could offer his services to people who had no money.

One case involved a woman who had been accused of writing bad checks. A large food chain had had her arrested. However, the company hadn't followed correct legal procedures. She should have been informed about the bad checks before her arrest. More importantly, she was innocent of the charges. Her ex-husband had forged her signature. The jury agreed that she had been treated unfairly under the law.[cxvi] Because she was awarded money, Harry was paid a percentage of what she received.

Juries

A jury is a group usually consisting of twelve adults who are selected to listen to the sworn evidence given in court and decide the verdict, or outcome. Lawyers for and against the person who is on trial will ask potential jury members questions, and, based on their answers, the lawyers select people to serve on the jury.

[cxiv] "What We Do," *Nevada Legal Services*, accessed June 16, 2015, http://nlslaw.net/what-we-do/.

[cxv] "How Does a Contingency Fee Agreement Work?," *Free Advice*, accessed June 16, 2015, http://law.freeadvice.com/litigation/litigation/lawyer_contingency_fee.htm.

[cxvi] Ibid., 157-159.

Members of the jury take an oath that they will give a fair verdict. Based upon the evidence, the jury decides whether someone is or is not guilty of breaking the law. When Harry began practicing law, women generally did not serve on juries.[cxvii]

Mike O'Callaghan wrote of how proud he felt when Harry "accepted his most courageous and, perhaps, most controversial civil case, representing a former classmate in a discrimination suit against the Clark County Sheriff's Department."[cxviii] The man, Larry Bolden, had done well on the tests to become a lieutenant with the sheriff's department. The only reason he was denied a promotion seemed to be that Bolden was black. Harry successfully argued that Bolden had been discriminated against. As a result, Bolden was promoted and eventually became the second-highest-ranking member of the Clark County force.[cxix]

[cvii] Marissa N. Batt, "Just Verdicts," *Ms. Magazine*, Summer 2004, http://www.msmagazine.com/summer2004/justverdicts.asp.

[cviii] Mike O'Callaghan, Forward to *Searchlight: The Camp That Didn't Fail*, by Harry Reid (Reno: University of Nevada Press, 1998), XV.

[cxix] Ibid.

WAS IT MURDER?

I N ONE OF his most famous cases, Harry represented a murderer. The evidence in the case indicated that the man was guilty. After talking to the suspected murderer, Harry felt the young man was innocent. Something about the case just didn't make sense to him. Lawyers often develop instincts about their clients' guilt or innocence.

A well-known Las Vegas couple, Martin and Emmalyn Payne, had moved to a home near Jackson Hole, Wyoming. Sometime later, they went missing. Blood was later found in their home and in their vehicle. Because of the blood, the police thought the Paynes had been murdered. The obvious suspect was their son, Russell. Without having found the bodies, the police weren't ready to charge Russell with murder. Instead, the police arrested him for driving under the influence of alcohol (DUI).

Russell was scared. He suspected the DUI charge against him would likely be changed to that of murder. Citizens in Jackson Hole, suspecting him of murder, had tried to kill him. Russell called Reid, who had helped him with prior legal matters in Nevada. He begged Harry to come quickly and "bring protection."

Anyone who would try to defend Russell would possibly have a difficult time proving he was innocent.

Harry Reid arrived in Wyoming eager to help Russell. However, Harry was only licensed to practice in Nevada. Someone with a Wyoming license would need to take care of legal details. Ted Frome, a local lawyer, agreed to help. Frome arranged for Russell's bail, which is the amount paid to the court to allow a person to leave jail. The money serves as a guarantee that the person will appear before the court. The money isn't returned if the person flees. Russell's bail was set at $10,000 (which is the equivalent of about $74,000 today) for his DUI arrest, the only charge against him at the time.

After the bail was paid, Russell was free. Since he had been arrested for the DUI offense, he could leave Wyoming. Harry wanted him out of the state before his parents' bodies were found. For a while, Russell would be safe from threats and attempts on his life. However, if the bodies were found and Russell was accused of murder, he would have to return to Wyoming for trial.

The next part of the story sounds like an episode from a TV program or a movie script.

Harry bought four plane tickets from Wyoming to Las Vegas. The authorities believed one ticket was Russell's.

Harry arrived at the airport alone. The authorities stopped him. They asked where Russell was. Harry said he didn't know, and it was true that he didn't. In the meantime, Russell's friends, who had raised the bail money, drove Russell, a possible murder suspect, to Idaho. There, Russell boarded a private plane to Las Vegas. He was safely out of Wyoming.

The defense team, led by Harry began to uncover as much information as it could. The evidence looked damaging for Russell. A miracle might be needed. Amazingly, late in the investigation, some important information was uncovered.

First, Harry arranged for Russell, whom the police believed to be a murder suspect, to see a psychiatrist. After submitting to various tests, Russell was found sane.

To complicate matters, Russell passed a polygraph test, indicating that he was innocent. So far, Harry's instincts seemed good.

Polygraph Tests

A polygraph test may also be called a "lie detector." A person who takes a polygraph test has a number of sensors attached to his or her body. The sensors measure the person's breathing rate, pulse, and blood pressure, among other things. Initially, the subject is asked a series of questions about himself. This allows the operators to see what the normal patterns of breath, heart rate, etc. are for the person being tested. Then, investigators ask questions about the topic at hand. It is believed that these patterns change when a person tells a lie.

By comparing the responses with those of the first, "normal" patterns, experienced polygraph operators can see when a person seems to be telling the truth or when the person is lying. Some people can "pass" polygraph tests when they are lying. Therefore, the results of polygraph tests are not used in courts today. They do, however, help lawyers decide how truthful their clients have been.[cxx]

Lawyers need to know as much as possible about their clients, so the psychiatrist continued to evaluate Russell. He checked Russell's medications. A medication called Deaner had been prescribed to Russell by his father, who was an orthopedic surgeon. At the time, Deaner was thought to be a cure for alcoholism. Russell drank excessively, and this would sometimes cause him to black out for days. When Dr. Payne had prescribed the medicine, Russell had agreed to take it.

While Russell remained in Las Vegas, the State of Wyoming charged him with murder. Although the police hadn't found the bodies, they had decided to proceed anyway. The facts that the Paynes were still missing and blood had been found in their home supported such charges. The state filed papers asking the State of Nevada to extradite, or return, Russell to

[cxx] "The Truth About Lie Detectors (aka Polygraph Tests)," *American Psychological Association*, accessed April 22, 2015, http://www.apa.org/research/action/polygraph.aspx.

Wyoming. Authorities intended to put Russell on trial in Jackson Hole. Harry needed to slow down the extradition process by making sure the paperwork had been done properly. Lawyers often check extradition papers carefully. A person's return can be delayed if papers have been drawn up incorrectly. During a delay, a lawyer might discover new information.

What Harry heard from sources in Jackson Hole was frightening. Each night, crowds gathered in the town square. There, they watched a stuffed figure, which was made to look like Russell, being hanged. If Russell were to return, could he be hanged by the crowd without a trial? His lawyers didn't want to chance it. Any delay would be to Russell's advantage.

Meanwhile, investigators researched the effects of the medication that Russell took.

Bingo! They found an article about Deaner's effects. In high doses, it could produce epileptic seizures. Few professionals were aware of this effect. A seizure occurs when too much energy passes through the brain. With serious seizures, people have uncontrollable movements lasting a minute or two. According to the article, some people on Deaner had shown very violent behavior. When questioned, they were unaware of their violent actions. Had the missing piece of the puzzle been found?

Epilepsy

Epilepsy is a condition caused by a "sudden surge of electrical activity in the brain."[cxxi] An epileptic seizure is classified by how much and which part of the brain is involved. A seizure can be mild, appearing as if a person has dozed off for a few seconds. In more frightening cases, a person may shake uncontrollably.[cxxii] About 10 percent of people may have epileptic seizures in their

---

[cxxi] "What is a Seizure?" *Epilepsy Foundation*, accessed April 22, 2015, http://www.epilepsy.com/learn/epilepsy-101/what-seizure.

[cxxii] "Epilepsy: Fact Sheet," *World Health Organization*, accessed May, 2015, http://www.who.int/mediacentre/factsheets/fs999/en/.

lifetimes.[cxxiii] Julius Caesar and Napoleon Bonaparte are two generals who suffered from epilepsy. Also, the great artists Leonardo da Vinci and Michelangelo were both thought to have had epilepsy. Both James Madison and Theodore Roosevelt, two United States presidents, suffered from epilepsy.[cxxiv]

Medications can help control epileptic episodes.

To find out whether this was the key to the Paynes' murders, doctors tested Russell. Would he exhibit violent behavior under the influence of Deaner? They began with a low dose, and slowly they increased it. The EEG, or brain scan, on Russell showed an irregular pattern. After doctors gave alcohol to Russell, the pattern became more irregular. Russell grew violent and needed to be restrained. Doctors concluded that the combination of alcohol and Deaner would produce violent actions in Russell. He seemed to be unaware of these actions. It had taken time, but Harry had the evidence he needed for the trial.

At about the same time, hunters near Jackson Hole found the missing bodies. An examination indicated that the Paynes had been shot and brutally attacked. Whoever had killed them seemed to have superhuman strength.

People around Jackson Hole now wondered how Russell could have killed his parents. He had been seen at home the night his parents had gone missing. It would have been impossible for him to travel the area, which included both a swamp and a dense forest, in such a short time. The authorities were puzzled.

Harry, too, was puzzled. He ordered another test. This time, Russell was given "truth serum" (see sidebar below). When he was questioned, the facts emerged. Russell Payne admitted to killing his parents. He told the

[cxxiii] "Epilepsy Stats and Facts," *Epilepsy Foundation*, accessed April 22, 2015, http://www.epilepsy.com/connect/forums/living-epilepsy-adults/epilepsy-stats-and-facts.

[cxxiv] "Famous People with Epilepsy," *Disabled World*, accessed April 22, 2015, http://www.disabled-world.com/artman/publish/epilepsy-famous.shtml.

interviewers that he hadn't planned to do it, that the gun had just gone off. Under the influence of the truth serum, Russell described his attacks on his parents. Now, no doubt remained about the Paynes' murderer. How would a judge and jury react to the information?

Truth Serum

What's called "truth serum" is usually either the drug sodium amytal or sodium pentothal.

In Russell's case, whichever was given revealed the truth.

Doctors discovered a so-called truth serum in the early 1900s. It was believed that the serum caused people to say what was really on their minds. As scientists experimented with truth serum, they had concerns. Some scientists feared that people who spoke under the influence of the sodium amytal or sodium pentothal might just be repeating words suggested to them. Therefore, they wouldn't necessarily be telling the truth about events.

Rarely has information obtained from truth serum been used in court. Today, most experts don't believe that truth serum is actually a way to get the truth, believing instead that it just seems to make people more talkative. What they say, though, may not be the truth.[cxxv]

Russell was tried for manslaughter, not murder. Manslaughter is a verdict given when a death is ruled accidental rather than intentional. He was found guilty and given a twenty-year sentence. The judge agreed to reduce Russell's sentence if future EEG exams were normal. Since they were, Russell served only six years. After being released from prison, Russell stayed out of trouble. Because he had not been found guilty of murder, Russell was able to legally inherit his parents' fortune.

[cxxv] Brenden Borrell, "What is Truth Serum?," *Scientific American*, December 4, 2008, http://www.scientificamerican.com/article/what-is-truth-serum/.

Harry and another lawyer who worked on the case received large fees. The team who had worked with Harry on the case put in the time and energy to pursue every angle. Their hard work saved Russell's life.[cxxvi]

 How would you handle a difficult situation in which you were accused of doing something you had not done? What if a teacher accused you of cheating or not turning in your homework? What if someone accused you of taking something you hadn't taken?

The first book Harry wrote was about the Payne murder case. He never published it.

[cxxvi] Reid, *The Good Fight*, 161-194.

A TRY AT ELECTED OFFICE

WHILE WORKING ON Russell Payne's case, Harry served in the Nevada legislature. It wasn't his first elected position after college. Why had he become involved in politics? Maybe he had always wanted to run for office. Perhaps Mike O'Callaghan's involvement in the politics of the Democratic Party sparked his interest. But neither had been the reason Harry had first run. Rather, an insult first encouraged him to seek office.

Harry had been asked to represent a doctor whose ethics had been questioned by the Clark County Hospital Board of Directors. Harry and the doctor had appeared before the board. According to Harry, the committee chairperson had said, "We do what we want to do." Harry was annoyed at the chairman's attitude and ran against him in his next board race. Harry won. From 1966 to 1968, Harry served as chair of the hospital board.[cxxvii]

Then, Harry set his goals higher. He ran for a legislative seat in the 1968 Nevada Assembly. As part of his campaign, he promised to improve the bad telephone service in Clark County. People liked what he'd had to say. Harry won by more votes than any of the other eighteen candidates from Clark County that year. He became one of two new members elected to the assembly that year.[cxxviii]

[cxxvii] K.J. Evans, "Harry Reid," *Las Vegas Review Journal*, September 12, 1999, http://www.reviewjournal.com/news/harry-reid.
[cxxviii] Ibid.

Legislators meet for only a few months every other year, and their pay is minimal, so Harry continued practicing law while he held this position.

While in the assembly, he worked to pass laws to protect the environment and to help consumers. He worked on bills to fight crime. Harry wrote, "I hold the record for introducing more bills in a session than any one person in history." However, he says, "I didn't get many of them passed, though."[cxxix]

Harry recalls one funny incident. After writing a bill pertaining to firefighters, he bragged to senate leaders about how good it was. The leader of the Nevada Senate agreed. Then he added that the "proposed" firefighting law was so good that the senate had already passed it.[cxxx] Harry learned to do his homework more thoroughly before proposing a bill.

Nevada Assembly

The Nevada State Legislature meets every two years and consists of two houses. The assembly is known as "the lower house." The senate is called "the upper house." The assembly has forty-two members, and the senate has twenty-one. Members of the assembly serve two-year terms, while senators serve four years.

**Figure 24: "Nevada Legislature Building, Carson City.
Nov. 1, 2007."**

[cxxix] Ibid.
[cxxx] Reid, *The Good Fight*, 222.

WINNING AND LOSING

WHAT WOULD HARRY do after his term ended in 1970? Would he run again for a seat in the state legislature? Would he seek another position? Thanks to O'Callaghan, Harry had another option. Mike O'Callaghan planned to run for governor, so Harry considered the job of lieutenant governor. In Nevada, the governor and lieutenant governor are elected separately. It is possible for them to be from different political parties, but the two might then have a difficult time working together. O'Callaghan and Harry, though, ran as democrats.

Both won. Harry's margin of victory was greater than that of O'Callaghan. Could this be a reward for the hard work Harry had done as an assemblyman? At 30, Harry became the youngest lieutenant governor in the United States and the youngest in Nevada history.[cxxxi] At first, his future seemed promising, but his hopes for holding other political offices ran into trouble.

Figure 25: Lieutenant Governor Harry Reid.

[cxxxi] Ibid., 223.

What's a Lieutenant Governor?

A lieutenant governor's job is in some ways like that of vice president of the United States. He does what the governor asks. He is the head of the state when the governor is away. He becomes governor if for some reason the governor can no longer serve. The lieutenant governor is president of the state senate. He also serves as the chair of the committee on Tourism and Economic Development.[cxxxii]

As lieutenant governor, Harry met one of his heroes, boxer Muhammad Ali, while Ali was in Las Vegas training for his upcoming heavyweight match. On June 27, 1972, Ali and Jerry Quarry would fight for the title of World Heavyweight Boxing Champion. Ali went on to win, and after that match, people called Ali "The Greatest" or "The Champ." He is still called that today.

Muhammad Ali

Muhammad Ali was born with the name Cassius Clay in January 1942. His interest in fighting began when he was 12. His bike had been stolen, and he wanted to beat up the thief, so he learned to box. He won his first match. Two years later, he earned the title of Golden Gloves Champion (Golden Gloves are amateur boxers).

In 1960, Clay was named to the U.S. Olympic Boxing Team. He won the gold medal and felt proud to represent the United States. The feeling didn't last long. Even though he was a returning hero, restaurants in his hometown of Louisville, Kentucky, refused to serve him.

This was because, at the time, restaurants and other businesses were segregated. Black people could not eat in the same

---

[cxxxii] State of Nevada Legislative Counsel Bureau, "Office of Lieutenant Governor Audit Report," May 2, 2008, http://www.leg.state.nv.us/Division/Audit/Full/documents/OfficeofLieutenantGovernorLA08-18FULL.pdf.

restaurants as whites. As a black man, he had represented the U.S. in the Olympics, which had been held in Rome. Yet Clay wasn't respected in his own country.

Some say that he was so angry over the incident, he threw his medal in the Ohio River (some people claim that he only lost it).[cxxxiii]

He became a professional fighter in 1960 and won his early fights. Within a few years, he had matches with the most famous fighters of the time, including Sonny Liston, Jerry Quarry, Joe Frazier, George Foreman, Leon Spinks, and Larry Holmes.

After joining the Black Muslims, known also as the Nation of Islam (NOI), in 1964, Cassius Clay changed his name to Cassius X, then to Muhammad Ali, the name by which he is known. He liked that NOI combined "elements of traditional Islam with black nationalist ideas."[cxxxiv] Among its many teachings, the black nationalist movement encouraged African-Americans to become business owners and form a black nation. By 2000, most of the members of NOI practiced the ideals of Islam and not of the black nationalist movement.

Some African-Americans, like Cassius Clay, changed their last names to "X." They reasoned that their last names had been given to them by slave owners, and, therefore, their true last names were unknown.[cxxxv]

Elijah Muhammad, the leader of NOI until his death in 1975, gave Cassius X the name Muhammad Ali. The name means "beloved of Allah." Allah is the name of the god worshipped by Islamic people.[cxxxvi] Islam was spread by the prophet Muhammad in the 7th century.[cxxxvii]

[cxxxiii] "Muhammad Ali Biography," *Internet Movie Database*, accessed April 27, 2015, http://www.imdb.com/name/nm0000738/bio.

[cxxxiv] John Gordon Melton, "Nation of Islam," *Encyclopaedia Britannica*, accessed April 27, 2015, http://www.britannica.com/EBchecked/topic/295614/Nation-of-Islam.

[cxxxv] Ibid.

[cxxxvi] "Muhammad Ali Biography," *Encyclopedia of World Biography*, accessed April 27, 2015, http://www.notablebiographies.com/A-An/Ali-Muhammad.html.

[cxxxvii] Fazlur Rahman, "Islam," *Encyclopaedia Britannica*, last modified June 17, 2015, http://www.britannica.com/topic/Islam.

After he beat Sonny Liston by a knockout, Muhammad Ali began to call himself "The Greatest," an epithet that has stuck with him ever since, even though he did lose a few fights. Boxers can win their fights with either a decision from the referees or when the other boxer is knocked down and doesn't rise by the count of ten. In sixty-one fights, Ali lost four of them and was knocked out only once.[cxxxviii]

Like some youths of the 1960s, he objected to the war in Vietnam. He was found guilty of refusing to serve in the military. Many didn't understand how he could be a fighter and yet refuse to fight in a war. As part of his punishment, he was banned from boxing for three and a half years. Years later, after a long, expensive court battle, his name was cleared and he was allowed to return to the ring.[cxxxix]

He will always be known as one of the world's greatest boxers.

Figure 26: "Muhammad Ali."

Figure 27:
"Portrait of Muhammad Ali, 1967."

[cxxxviii] "Muhammad Ali's Ring Record," *ESPN Classic*, November 19, 2003, http://espn.go.com/classic/s/Ali_record.html.

[cxxxix] Muhammad Ali Biography," *A&E Television Networks, LLC.*, accessed June 9, 2015, http://www.biography.com/people/muhammad-ali-9181165.

Figure 28: "Muhammad Ali (right) fights Joe Frazier."

 What famous person would you like to meet? Would it be a sports figure, a musician, a movie star, or maybe the president of the United States? Would it be someone from the past? What would you chat about?

Harry met with Ali a few days before his fight with Quarry. For an hour and a half, the two talked about boxing and Ali's diet. But the excitement of meeting Ali was short-lived. The day ended as one of the worst in Harry's life.

At his office, at around noon, Harry spoke to his mother, who had called with terrible news.

"Your pop shot himself,"[cxl] she told him. Harry's father had only been 57 years old.

Harry called his brothers and then drove to Searchlight. His father's body was still on the bed, covered in blood. Mother and son waited for officials to arrive from Las Vegas. After Harry, Sr.'s body was taken to a funeral home, Harry, Jr. returned to his office, where his coworkers hugged him and asked questions. Harry couldn't talk about his father's suicide. It hurt too much.

[cxl] Reid, *The Good Fight*, 231.

Harry didn't understand his father's action. Had the older man's worsening health been the cause? Had it been the untreated depression from which he had suffered after he'd quit drinking? The Reid family would never know. For years, Harry would not talk about it.

When Harry helped his mother file insurance papers, he discovered that his parents had not actually been married when he and his brother Larry had been born.[cxli] Harry had already known that Don and Dale were his stepbrothers. Now, Harry realized he and Larry were illegitimate. Before the 1960s, children who were born out of wedlock were often called "bastards," a term that meant that they were illegitimate; such people were often treated as outcasts. Many people even considered them to be inferior to children who were born within a marriage. Often, illegitimate children couldn't inherit money or property. Even worse, they were bullied. Fortunately, neither of the boys seemed to have experienced such comments.

Two months after his father's suicide, Harry and Landra had their fourth child, a boy named Josh. Harry busied himself in his work as lieutenant governor. Life returned to normal—at least, normal for the Reids.

After serving as lieutenant governor, Harry's political plans depended on those of Mike O'Callaghan. Mike thought he would run for a United States Senate seat; Harry decided he would campaign for governor. At the last minute, however, O'Callaghan changed his mind. He would seek the governor's office again. Now, Harry had to make an important decision. Would he run for lieutenant governor or choose to do something else? After much thought, he decided to run for the senate seat that O'Callaghan had considered.

For most of the senate race, Harry was ahead of his opponent in the polls. It looked as if he would win. Throughout the country, Democrats like himself were doing well because Republican President Richard Nixon had resigned from office, in the wake of a scandal called Watergate that had brought Nixon down.

[cxli] Ibid., 233.

Watergate

Watergate is the name of an office complex in Washington, D.C., and it became the name of a political scandal that caused Richard Nixon, the 37th president of the United States, to resign in August 1974.

The scandal began when five men were arrested for breaking into Democratic National Committee headquarters at the Watergate complex. Tape recordings revealed that the president had tried to cover up the break-in, as well as other illegal activities meant to gather information about political opponents. A legal ruling required Nixon to give up the tapes to authorities. Instead, he resigned because, otherwise, he was likely to be impeached— that is, removed from office by the U.S. Congress. After Nixon resigned, his vice president, Gerald Ford, became the 38th president.[cxlii]

Despite Watergate and the success of Democrats, Harry lost the election to Paul Laxalt by six hundred votes. Harry and his campaign workers had made mistakes, the worst of which had been to attack the finances of members of the Laxalt family. One member of the family had been a nun; Catholic nuns take a vow of poverty and own few personal items.[cxliii] This attack had not been viewed favorably. Nevadans had shown with their votes that they preferred former Governor Laxalt.

Did this reveal a dislike of Harry's campaign techniques? Would voters still support Harry in future elections? Harry wondered what he would do next.

After losing the senate seat, Harry ran for mayor of Las Vegas. He campaigned well, and it looked as if he would be the next mayor. On election night, Harry led in the vote count. In Nevada, as in many states, a

cxlii History Channel, "This Day in History, August 8: 1974, Nixon Resigns," *A&E Television Networks, LLC.*, accessed June 16, 2015, http://www.history.com/this-day-in-history/nixon-resigns.
cxliii Ibid., 234-235.

candidate must receive more than 50 percent of the vote. Unfortunately, he had fewer than the necessary 50 percent to win outright. The two candidates with the highest percentages, Harry Reid and Bill Briar, participated in a run-off election. Harry lost by more than 5 percent of the votes.[cxliv]

After losing two major campaigns, most politicians would call it quits. Harry's losses had come within seven months of each other. Campaigning for office is expensive and time consuming. Would he want to run again? Also, people give money to candidates so that they can pay for their campaigns; they would think carefully about supporting someone who had lost twice.

Not surprisingly, Harry chose not to run for office again. Instead, Governor O'Callaghan appointed him to his next position, naming Harry the head of the Nevada Gaming Commission.

However, the job almost cost him his reputation and his life. The lives of Harry's wife and their five children—four sons and daughter ranging in age from three to sixteen—were also put in danger. When Harry accepted the job, of course, he didn't know the risk to his family or himself.

Harry had talked with the man who had held the job before him, and the former commissioner told Harry about threats that had been made to his life. Harry believed the man was just imagining the threats. Eventually, though, he would find out that the former commissioner had had reasons to be afraid. Harry took the job without knowing what to expect.

Harry knew little about how casinos were run. He had actually never gone into a casino to gamble. He didn't realize to what degree gangsters were in control of the gaming world. Such control wasn't apparent to most people, although many suspected it.

[cxliv] Ibid., 235.

Nevada Gaming Commission

The Gaming Commission oversees gambling in Nevada. The commission is in charge of enforcing the rules, giving licenses to gaming establishments, and providing discipline to those who are not following the rules. Those serving on the committee serve four years.[cxlv]

[cxlv] "Gaming Commission," *Nevada Gaming Control Board*, accessed June 16, 2015, http://gaming.nv.gov/index. aspx?page=3.

THE FBI, EX-TEXAS RANGERS,
GANGSTERS, AND BOMB THREATS

WHAT HAPPENED WHEN Harry was head of the commission sounds like another television or movie script, complete with gangsters and death threats. In fact, one event that took place during his time on the commission was used in the 1995 movie *Casino*. The movie's screenwriters used the dialogue from court testimony.

Harry in the Movies?

Harry has had small roles in two movies. In 2000, he was in *Traffic*, a well-reviewed movie about U.S./Mexican drug problems. Several other politicians also had parts.

He and Senators Barack Obama and Sam Brownback also appeared in the 2007 documentary movie *Sand and Sorrow*, about the civil war in the North African country of Darfur.[cxlvi] Estimates say that by March 2003, anywhere from 63,000 to almost 150,000 died in the fighting there or from starvation and illness.[cxlvii] The movie called attention to the horrors of the war being waged against non-Arabs in western Sudan.

The Nevada Gaming Commission ensures that laws pertaining to the gaming industry are enforced. The public must have confidence that games haven't been fixed or controlled.

[cxlvi] "Harry Reid," *Internet Movie Database*, accessed April 27, 2015, http://www.imdb.com/name/nm0717285/.
[cxlvii] "Sudan: Death Toll in Darfur," *U.S. Department of State*, accessed April 27, 2015, http://2001-2009.state.gov/s/inr/rls/fs/2005/45105.htm.

One job of the commission is to make certain that employees don't have criminal records. This is why anyone who applies to work in a casino must undergo a background check. If a person is found guilty of violating laws, that person's name is placed in the "Black Book." Those whose names are in the book can't even enter a casino. If they do, armed guards escort them out. When Harry served on the commission, many names in the book were those of suspected gangsters. Casinos were an easy way for such people to make money.

An important role of the commission is to approve new games, to ensure that they are run fairly, and are not rigged in favor of a casino. If a game was not authorized, an interested party might try to get someone in the commission to change his mind by using illegal methods.

Jack Gordon, a wealthy man in the entertainment business, ran into problems with the Nevada Gaming Commission. He had ideas for two games, which he thought could earn him millions. At first, he followed the proper process to implement these games, but the commission didn't approve them. A game can be rejected for many reasons. In Gordon's case, the commission felt his proposed games favored the casino too much.

Gordon needed a different strategy, even if it were illegal, so that he could get his games played in casinos. He decided to pressure someone to give him what he wanted, and he thought the commission head, Harry Reid, would be good choice. In Gordon's mind, a young lawyer could, undoubtedly, use money. Gordon offered Harry a $12,000 bribe to approve the games.

 Where do you think ideas for crime movies come from? Are they from the writers' imaginations? Are they based upon things that have actually happened? Do you think truth is stranger than fiction?

Harry called in the FBI. Agents attached audio equipment wires to Harry that enabled them to listen in on the conversation between him and

Gordon. The FBI would also need evidence of the $12,000 bribe. Otherwise, Gordon could claim that he had never offered it. Officials would then have a difficult time winning a court case.

Harry and the agents worked out a plan. When Harry said, "Is this the money?" they would enter Harry's office and arrest Gordon. The two men talked, and Gordon offered Harry the money. The plan was going just as Harry and the FBI had hoped until Harry said, "Is this the money?" The FBI did not appear. Harry repeated the words, and still the agents didn't enter.

Eventually, the FBI broke down the door. Neither Harry nor the agents had been aware that Gordon had locked the outside door.

Harry was furious that Gordon had thought he could be bribed. In fact, he was so angry that the FBI officers had to hold Harry back from hitting Gordon.

A court of law found Gordon guilty of attempting to bribe an official.[cxlviii]

Later, Harry and his family began to receive death threats.

Bomb threats were also made against the office building where Harry worked. Workers were forced to leave the building while police checked carefully. No bombs were ever found.

Would whoever had made the threats actually bomb Harry's office? Was this person checking how thoroughly the police were following through on threats? Would he try something else? Harry didn't have to wait long for the answer.

One day, Harry's wife, Landra, felt something was wrong with their car. Thinking that Landra's complaints were strange, Harry called the police.

They searched and found a bomb under the hood. Fortunately for the Reids, the bomb had not been hooked up correctly. From then on, Landra and Harry started their cars with remote controls. Whether or not Gordon was involved in the bombing remains a mystery.[cxlix]

Another time, Harry was the accused. The FBI had a taped conversation of a criminal who claimed he was bribing a "Mr. Cleanface." No one

---

[cxlviii] Reid, *The Good Fight*, 237-242.
[cxlix] Ibid., 247-252, 256, 270.

knew who "Mr. Cleanface" was. Some people thought Harry fit the description. As soon as FBI agents heard the tape, they asked the court's permission to listen in on Harry's phone calls.

Meanwhile, the Nevada Gaming Commission hired two retired Texas Rangers (a Texas law enforcement agency) to investigate. They investigated Harry's finances. They wanted to know where any amount of money over $250 came from or how it was spent. This included Landra's grocery money, Harry's law office finances, and all of Harry's personal finances. The Rangers were thorough, even checking the Reids' children's savings accounts. As part of the inquiry, they followed Harry to see what he did all day. Nothing suspicious was seen.

When Harry heard the accusation, he intended to clear his name. He volunteered to take a polygraph test, and, after careful examination, he was cleared. No one ever figured out who "Mr. Cleanface" might have been.[d] Some have even suggested that the criminal had talked about a "Mr. Cleanface" to impress others.

Harry's four-year term on the commission ended in 1981. He returned to his law practice but didn't stay long. People had been impressed with his work on the commission. Could he now win a congressional seat? Was there even a seat he could run for? A Democrat held Nevada's only seat in the House of Representatives. Harry wasn't likely to run against a fellow Democrat. Again, Harry Reid was lucky.

---

[d] Ibid., 247, 257-263.

PART 4

D.C., ANOTHER TRY?

BACK TO WASHINGTON

A STATE'S POPULATION determines the number of members it sends to the House of Representatives in Washington, D.C. Every state is entitled to at least one representative. Before 1982, Nevada was one of the states that sent just one member to the House. Nevada's population, especially in the Las Vegas area, had grown in the 1970s. Therefore, the state gained a second seat in the 1982 election. Now, one person would represent the northern part of the state, and a newly elected person would serve the southern part. Harry Reid won this southern seat.

Qualifications for House and Senate Seats

Article 1 of the United States Constitution states the requirements for members of the House and the Senate:

A person who is a representative must be at least 25 years old, a citizen of the U.S. for at least seven years, and a resident of the state in which the person is elected.

A senator must be at least 30 years old, a citizen for at least nine years, and a resident of the state in which the person is elected.

In 1787, at the time the U.S. Constitution was adopted, women, blacks, and American Indians couldn't vote. The 15th Amendment, ratified in 1870, allowed black males to vote. In

1920, the 19th Amendment granted voting rights to women. When legislation passed Congress in 1924 to give citizenship to American Indians, they, too, could vote.[cli]

When Harry's first term expired in 1984, he easily won re-election.

As Nevada's only Democrat in the House, Harry turned to California's Democrats for help. From them he learned how to be a more effective representative. The delegates welcomed him. Of course, this didn't mean he was becoming a Californian. It meant that, on Wednesdays, he attended strategy meetings with the Californians. During his second term in office, Harry was elected the secretary-treasurer of the group. Again, he sought advice from others in order to do a better job.

In the House, he worked to protect Nevada's wilderness areas. Through his efforts as well as those of others, Great Basin National Park was born. The 77,180-acre park,[clii] with its unusual environment, was established in 1986. Some of its almost 5,000-year-old bristlecone pines are the longest-living trees and may well be the oldest living things in the world.[cliii]

Figure 29: "Rare bristlecone pine at Great Basin National Park."

[cli] Sandra Brown, "America the Beautiful: A History of the Right to Vote in the US," *League of Women Voters, Albuquerque-Bernalillo County*, last modified April 7, 2005, http://www.lwvabc.org/pubs/history_of_vote.html.

[clii] National Park Service, "Great Basin National Park," *National Park Service Land Resources Division Listing of Acreage (Summary)*, last modified December 31, 2011, https://irma.nps.gov/Stats/DownloadFile/107.

[cliii] "Bristlecone Pines," Great Basin National Park Nevada, *National Park Service*, last modified September 24, 2015, http://www.nps.gov/grba/planyourvisit/identifying-bristlecone-pines.htm.

Lehman Caves, with nearly two miles of passageways, have stalactites and stalagmites like those seen in many caves. But unlike most caves, Lehman's contain many unusual formations. Among its unusual cave decorations are helictites. These formations curve upward, defying gravity. "The diversity of formations in Lehman Caves is so great, that one would have to travel countless caves to see everything that can be seen on a 60-minute tour of the cave system." [cliv]

Figure 30: "Wheeler Peak, the tallest peak in Nevada, is inside Great Basin National Park."

Figure 31: "Parachute Shield, the most famous shield in Lehman Caves."

[cliv] "Speleothems (Cave Formations)," Great Basin National Park Nevada, *National Park Service*, September 19, 2012, http://www.nps.gov/grba/learn/nature/speleothems-cave-formations.htm.

Figure 32: "Column and drapery formations found in Lehman Caves."

Figure 33: "An abundance of speleothems are revealed in each room of Lehman Caves."

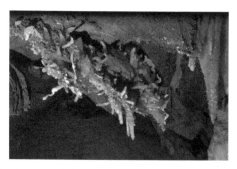

Figure 34: "Helictites defying gravity, in the West Room of Lehman Caves."

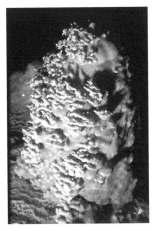

Figure 35: "Stalagmite ornately decorated in Lehman Caves."

Figure 36: "A rare moment when water is forced under pressure through a soda straw formation."

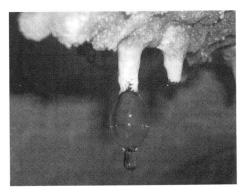

Figure 37: "On rare occasions, bubbles appear on soda straws for a short period of time, usually in early spring."

The park also has six lakes and miles of trails for hiking, mountain biking, or skiing.

Especially because of its beauty and many unique traits, Great Basin needed this protection by the federal government.

When Harry received an award for helping maintain land for future generations, he said, "Through these actions, we leave our children and grandchildren the opportunity to see the full bounty of nature. It is a great honor to receive this award, and to have the privilege to work with the people of Nevada to protect some of our state's most wild and sacred areas."[clv]

As senator, Harry continued his interest in preserving land. He helped create three new units of the park system.

The National Parks

"Creating national parks and setting aside wild lands for public enjoyment is a uniquely American idea," Harry has said. "National parks have now been created all over the world, but they started here in the United States with President Abraham Lincoln. . . ."[clvi]

Seven years after the Civil War ended, a Union general was elected President of the United States. While president, General Ulysses S. Grant officially established Yellowstone, the first National Park, in March of 1872. The idea of protecting land in this way had actually come from President Lincoln. On June 30, 1864, Lincoln named Yosemite Valley and the Mariposa Grove of Giant Sequoias in California an area to "be held for public use."[clvii]

In 1916, President Woodrow Wilson signed the act that created the National Park Service. Since that first park, Yellowstone, the park service has grown to include over 397 different areas.

[clv] "Reid Given Top Award for Defending National Parks," Press Release, *United States Senator for Nevada Harry Reid*, April 2, 2009, http://www.reid.senate.gov/press_releases/reid-given-top-award-for-defending-national-parks.

[clvi] Ibid.

[clvii] "About – Yosemite 125th Anniversary/NPS," *National Park Service*, accessed May 20, 2015, http://www.nps.gov/featurecontent/yose/anniversary/about/index.html.

The White House is one of those areas. Others include parks like Yellowstone, as well as monuments, battlefields, and historic sites. These areas range from a two-hundred-acre memorial in Pennsylvania to a 13.2-million-acre park and preserve in Alaska. In 2010, almost 300 million people visited one of these. The National Park Service website (http://www.nps.gov/news/upload/NPS-Park-Listing_11-7-11.pdf) contains a complete list of national parks.

An arrowhead emblem is used to represent the National Park Service (NPS) as its logo. The arrowhead shape looks like it could have been dug from an ancient site. On the arrowhead is the outline of a white bison, representing wildlife; behind and to the left can be seen a large sequoia tree. Other trees, water, and snow-capped mountains complete the scene in the NPS logo.

Figure 38: "The emblem of the National Park Service."

Harry was ambitious and felt he could better serve Nevadans in a different position. So after two terms in the House, he decided to seek higher office. He ran for a Senate seat.

How Congress Became the Way it is

The Founding Fathers wrote the Articles of Confederation. These were the rules by which the new nation would operate. Under the Articles, the central government couldn't fight wars, tax people for revenue, settle disagreements between states, or regulate commerce. Once the Articles were adopted, public officials realized this type of government wasn't working. They believed a strong central government was needed.

Therefore, major changes in the Articles had to be made. A Constitutional Convention was called in 1787 to create a different type of government. Fifty-five men attended the convention, including John Adams, Alexander Hamilton, James Madison, and George Washington. Even Benjamin Franklin attended, though he was so ill he had to be brought to the convention in a sedan chair.[clviii]

Men at the Constitutional Convention created three branches of government: the executive branch (the president's office), the judicial branch (the court system), and the legislative branch (the two houses of Congress).

One of the many debates was about how the legislative branch would work. Attendees had different beliefs based upon the sizes of the states from which they came. Some representatives, such as those from the large state of Virginia, wanted the number of members of Congress to be based on a state's population. Other delegates from smaller populations wanted each state to have an equal number of representatives. This major disagreement had to be resolved. And, in a unique way, it was.

The House of Representatives and the Senate were created. The House would select members based upon each state's population; the Senate would have two representatives from each state. This Great Compromise is the arrangement under which our government works today.[clix]

[clviii] National Archives and Records Administration, "The Founding Fathers Delegates to the Constitution Convention," *The Charters of Freedom "A New World Is At Hand,"* May 23, 2015, http://www.archives.gov/exhibits/charters/constitution_founding_fathers.html.

[clix] National Archives and Records Administration, "Constitution of the United States," *The Charters of Freedom "A New World Is At Hand,"* May 23, 2015, http://www.archives.gov/exhibits/charters/constitution.html.

Many other conflicts also had to be resolved. Another issue was how much power the central government should have. This issue still divides our nation.

Overall, the Constitutional Convention established a workable government for the new country.

Figure 39: "Scene at the Signing of the Constitution of the United States."

Everyone agreed that George Washington, the great military hero of the Revolutionary War, should be the first president.

Almost as soon as Congress was established, people with similar views began to work with each other on issues. This was the beginning of our two-party system. One faction wanted a strong central government, and another wanted the states to have more power.[clx]

The names and purposes of the parties have changed somewhat over the years, but a struggle between state and federal power is ongoing.

[clx] David K. Abraham, "A Brief History of the American Two Party System," accessed May 20, 2015, http://davidk-abraham.com/OldWeb/Beliefs/America/twopartysystem.htm.

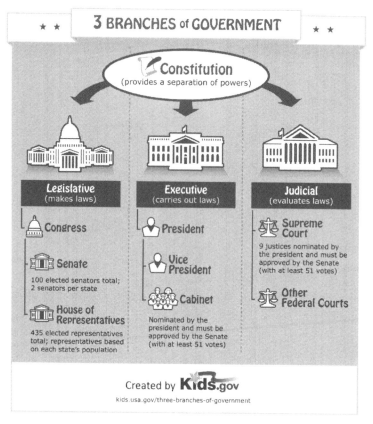

Figure 40: "Kids.gov Three Branches of Government Poster."

Harry Reid won the 1986 senatorial election by a large margin (50 percent to 44.5 percent). Soon after winning the election, he began to work on solving a problem that had existed for 100 years. The local governments of California and Nevada and the Paiute Indian Tribe had been involved in a dispute over a precious resource: water. Central to the dispute was how much access to water for drinking and farming each group should have. Each party felt it needed a larger share. It took Senator Reid until 2008 to help work out an agreement that was mutually agreeable to all.[clxi] As Secretary of the Interior

---

[clxi] Reid, *The Good Fight*, 274.

Dirk Kempthorne said on the day that the agreement was signed, "We now have an agreement that benefits all who depend on the river for water and ensures that the people of the states of California and Nevada can move forward with certainty to a more prosperous future. . . . [T]his day is part of a new day in the West." [clxii]

Harry ran for re-election to the Senate again in 1992. He won by an even larger margin (51 percent to 40 percent) than he had previously.

 A candidate who called himself "God Almighty" challenged Harry in the1992 primary. Do you think God Almighty was actually the person's name? At the time, Nevada allowed names like that on the ballot, but it no longer does.

Would you like to change your name? If so, what would it be? Why?

The November 3, 1998 election was close. Only 401 votes separated Harry from John Ensign, his Republican opponent. In fact, it was so close that it took a month to officially declare a winner. Ensign decided to pay $59,000 to have the votes recounted. The recount determined that Harry had 428 more votes than Ensign. On December 10, Harry was declared the winner. [clxiii] In 2000, Ensign won Nevada's second senate seat. Both men worked to help Nevadans.

Political parties help their candidates by providing voter lists and money and recruiting workers. Important party officials often give speeches, each praising their candidate. In 2004, Democrats supported Harry. However, not all Republicans stood by their nominee. Some openly supported Harry. That year, Harry won sixty-one percent of the vote.

---

clxii "Secretary Kempthorne Congratulates Senator Reid, Paiute Tribe, Federal and State Officials and Water Authority at Signing Ceremony for Truckee River Operating Agreement," News Release, *U.S. Department of the Interior*, November 9, 2008, http://www.doi.gov/news/archive/08_News_Releases/090808.html.

clxiii Reid, *The Good Fight*, 275-276.

Think about it! Why would prominent people in the opposing party support Harry? Does this say more about Harry or about his opponent? Should officials who have won election with various kinds of help from their party speak out against their party's candidate under certain circumstances? What might those be?

If you were running for a school office, would you vote for yourself? Why or why not? Should you vote for a friend just because the person is your friend? Why or why not?

When he first served in Congress, Harry received praise from both Democrats and Republicans. Over a decade ago, Republican Senator Mitch McConnell of Kentucky, the man who succeeded Harry as Majority Leader, said of Harry, "He's a straight shooter, smart and easy to work with. Having said that, I also know he can be a tough opponent."[clxiv] Another current Republican Senator, Orrin Hatch, a Mormon from Utah, once said, "We all respect Senator Reid. He is one of the moderate voices around here who tries to get things to work."[clxv] Today, both senators often speak out against Majority Leader Reid.

As Governor Mike O'Callaghan wrote in his forward, ". . .in 1993 *Parade Magazine* listed Harry as one of six senators known for their character and integrity."[clxvi] Harry is proud enough of the recognition that he includes it on his Senate website.

Chuck Schumer, a Democratic senator from New York, said of Harry, "His character and fundamental decency are at the core of why he's been such a successful and beloved leader. He's so respected by our caucus for his strength, his legislative acumen, his honesty, and his determination."[clxvii]

[clxiv] Doug Waller, "Herding the Democrats," *Time*, November 14, 2004, http://content.time.com/time/magazine/article/0,9171,782108,00.html.

[clxv] "About Senator Harry Reid," *United States Senator for Nevada Harry Reid*, accessed November 10, 2014, http://www.reid.senate.gov/about.

[clxvi] Mike O'Callaghan, Forward to *Searchlight: The Camp That Didn't Fail*, by Harry Reid, (Reno: University of Nevada Press, 1998), XI-XVII.

[clxvii] Carl Hulse, "Harry Reid to Retire from Senate in 2016," *The New York Times*, March 27, 2015, http://www.nytimes.com/2015/03/28/us/politics/senator-harry-reid-retire.html.

In time, Republicans altered their attitude toward him. Harry would be subject to many attacks on issues ranging from his ethics to his voting record. People began to question whether he should be in government. Why the change?

IMPORTANT JOBS AND TROUBLE

THE CHANGE WAS most likely caused by the important jobs Harry had held, trouble he had found himself in, and votes he had made on controversial issues.

From 1999 to 2005, Harry was Senate Democratic Whip. The whip is the assistant party leader. Whips persuade members of their party to vote along party lines. In other words, he "whips them" into shape. Whips are the third or fourth most powerful senators. Harry was good at whipping up votes for Democratic causes. Republicans were unhappy with his success. Their dislike grew as Harry became more powerful.

Between 2001 and 2003, he chaired the Senate Ethics Committee. Six members of each party serve on the committee. The Senate's majority party selects the chairperson. The committee's job is to check that each senator maintains acceptable behavior. It looks into charges made against a senator. Also, committee members investigate whether laws have been broken. They can suggest a punishment and, if needed, contact the police.

 Why would Congress need an ethics committee? Wouldn't people in the public eye behave themselves naturally?

If you were on an ethics committee at your school or place of worship, what would you watch out for?

The Ethics Committee frowns on senators receiving gifts. Their concern is that if a senator accepts a gift, he or she will be swayed to vote a certain way. Therefore, accepting meals or trips from lobbyists is considered unethical.

Harry learned firsthand about the problems resulting from accepting gifts. It was his interest in boxing that caused trouble. In May 2006, a report indicated Harry had accepted tickets to boxing matches from the Nevada Athletic Commission. These tickets issued between 2003 and 2005 allowed him to attend matches at no cost. Someone who had bought tickets would have paid hundreds of dollars for each of the three matches that Harry attended.

Was there a motive behind issuing the tickets to Harry? There may have been. The Senate planned to vote on creating a federal boxing commission. The Nevada Athletic Commission opposed a federal commission because its power might be weakened. Was the commission trying to influence Harry's vote? If so, it didn't work. Harry voted for the creation of a national commission.[clxviii]

The Ethics Committee started its investigation into whether Harry had violated Senate rules. He had accepted free tickets, but it turned out he had received special tickets called "credentials." These are provided only to public officials and have no monetary value.[clxix] To avoid future problems, Harry agreed to no longer accept gifts of that type. After this incident, his ethical behavior on various issues was examined more closely.

Lobbyists

A lobbyist is paid to sway a congressperson's opinion on an issue.

In the last few years, there have been over 10,000 lobbyists who

---

[clxviii] The Associated Press, "Senator Reid Admits Erring on Ethics Rule," *The New York Times*, June 2, 2006, http://www.nytimes.com/2006/06/02/washington/02reid.html?_r=0.

[clxix] Simon Maloy, "Even More Serious Flaws Emerge in ASP Story About Reid's Attendance at Boxing Matches," *Media Matters for America*, May 31, 2006, http://mediamatters.org/research/2006/05/31/even-more-serious-flaws-emerge-in-ap-story-abou/135839.

have spent more than $3 billion a year supporting their causes. The tech industry, defense contractors, and the National Rifle Association (NRA) are among the largest lobbying groups. Each of these groups has a position on an issue that it wants our representatives to support.

There is a lobby on almost every issue, from automobile safety to zoo regulations. Even bicyclists have a lobby. The American League of Bicyclists has pressured congressional representatives in support of safe routes to schools.

A lobbyist might merely talk to someone in order to persuade him. However, lobbyists have also bought meals, provided gifts, or arranged and paid for trips.[clxx]

What is your opinion of lobbyists? Are there some issues that only lobbyists can supply information about? How else could a congressperson learn about an issue?

Should someone in Congress be able to go out to lunch or dinner with a person who has information or opinions on an issue that will come up for a vote? What if the lobbyist is a good friend of a person in Congress?

[clxx] Rachel Cooper, "What is a Lobbyist? – FAQs About Lobbying," *About Travel*, accessed July 10, 2015, http://dc.about.com/od/jobs/a/Lobbying.htm.

BECOMING THE MOST IMPORTANT SENATOR

IN 2005, an opportunity arose for Harry to obtain a more important role in the Senate. Tom Daschle, a Democrat from South Dakota, lost his Senate election. Many senators were surprised at the loss. Daschle had been minority leader and worked closely with Harry, the Democratic whip.

Harry decided to seek the minority leader position. After the 2005 election, Democrats outnumbered Republicans in the Senate. The majority leader, therefore, would be a Democrat when senators began the new term in January 2006. At the beginning of each term, Republican and Democratic senators elect their leaders. Harry ran for majority leader and won. Because one-third of the Senate comes up for election every two years, a leadership position like this is held for two years.

Harry seems an unlikely person to hold a powerful position. He is not a particularly good speaker and shies away from talk shows. His voice is soft and hard to hear. Sometimes, he mumbles. Jon Ralston, a political analyst and writer in Nevada, has said that Harry is a "manifestly terrible candidate." [clxxi] He appears thin, a bit stooped, modest looking, or even meek. Therefore, people tend to misjudge him.

However, he has many skills that make him successful as a leader. He doesn't seem to care about how the public views him. As Jon Ralston

---

[clxxi] Jon Ralston, "Machiavelli With Malaprops," *Politico*, December 15, 2013, http://www.politico.com/magazine/story/2013/12/harry-reid-ralston-machiavelli-with-malaprops-101168.html#.

wrote, Harry spends "little effort tending his public image." [clxxii] The former majority leader listens to all the members of his party and tries to understand what they want. Senator Brown of Ohio said, "I think he leads us where we want to go." [clxxiii] Harry is "by nature a pragmatic deal-cutter" [clxxiv] and "a back-room deal maker." [clxxv] Ross Baker, a Rutgers University professor, said the following of Harry: "Behind the scenes, his genius really comes to the floor. He's a virtuoso, a legislative technician." [clxxvi]

Since Harry now led the Democratic Party, he was the person who spoke out against President George Herbert Walker Bush's policies. In his book, *The Good Fight: Hard Lessons from Searchlight to Washington*, Harry writes about his disagreements with the president on many issues. One issue, in particular, involved the use of Yucca Mountain, which is near Las Vegas and was built as a nuclear waste site. After Bush won the presidency in 2000, he favored using Yucca as a waste site, the opposite of the position he had taken when running for office.

 Think about it! Do you feel that people who run for office should only make statements that they feel they can keep? Would it be okay for a candidate to change his mind? In what situations?

Harry ran again in 2009 for the position of majority leader and won every vote. He continued in the job in 2011 and 2013. As majority leader, Harry was viewed by many in the Republican Party as an obstacle in getting its agenda passed. He was thought to be too close to President Obama,

[clxxii] Ibid.

[clxxiii] Jennifer Steinhauer, "As Views Shift on Guns, Reid Corrals Senate," *The New York Times*, March 31, 2013, http://www.nytimes.com/2013/04/01/us/politics/harry-reid-draws-on-political-calculus-as-he-leads-senate.html?hp.

[clxxiv] Adam Nagourney, "Reid Faces Battles in Washington and at Home," *The New York Times Magazine*, January 12, 2010, http://www.nytimes.com/2010/01/24/magazine/24reid-t.html?_r=0.

[clxxv] Ibid.

[clxxvi] Ibid.

who took office on January 20, 2009, when the economy was poor. Each party had its own idea of how to improve the economy. Democrats, led by Harry, and Republicans would blame the other party for the poor economy.

In his article in *The New York Times Magazine*, "Reid Faces Battles in Washington and at Home," Adam Nagourney writes "For all the power and the glamour—the personal relationship with a president, the corner office in the Capitol, the place in history—it is hard to see why anyone would want to be Harry Reid in today's Washington."[clxxvii] People in these positions, like Harry Reid, are important figures in their parties and in the country. They are the people who officially speak for their parties. Lawmakers like Harry represent their parties' views in discussions with the president, with the opposing party, and with the news media.

Members of each party work closely with their leaders. Together, they decide committee assignments, whom to confirm to office, appointments to jobs, the passage of bills, and when to take part in debates. The leaders of each party aid individual senators by helping them receive the committee assignments they want.

The majority leader has additional powers. The majority leader has the privilege of speaking first, so he can emphasize his party's ideas more effectively. The leader manages the order in which business is discussed on the Senate floor. He also decides on the order in which people speak. Most importantly, he can decide whether an issue even comes before the Senate. Republicans have not been happy that Harry has prevented many votes from coming to the Senate floor.

Leadership jobs also require work. Leaders need to be up to date on national and international matters. They need to know the details of each bill that is introduced. They are required to be on the floor of the Senate when it is in session to make sure procedures are followed. If one of them is absent, an appointee stands in.

[clxxvii] Ibid.

Harry has been considered very knowledgeable about Senate rules—an advantage in his role.

As the highest congressional official in President Obama's party, Harry helps the president with his legislative needs. Many of President Obama's policies have been unpopular among Republicans. Therefore, both the president and Harry receive criticism. According to *The Washington Post*'s "The U.S. Congress Voters Database," in the 112th Congress, Harry voted with the Democratic Party 95 percent of the time. Senator Mitch McConnell, the previous minority leader and new majority leader (as of 2015), has voted with his party 92 percent of the time. Only seven senators have voted less than 80 percent with their party.[clxxviii]

Because members of Congress usually vote along party lines, the 112th Congress (which ended in January 2013) passed only 284 bills, which is the worst record since 1974.[clxxix] To become a law, the president signs a bill once it has passed both the House and the Senate. In the 112th Congress, Republicans controlled the House, and Democrats the Senate. Different views held by members of each party often meant the two houses of Congress didn't agree on what to pass. So fewer than 300 bills came to the president for his signature.

Those who like less government interference in their lives may be content that fewer bills are sent to the president for his signature. They feel that bills signed by a Democratic president may call for more government spending, which they are against. However, many Americans don't view a reduced number as a good thing. Instead, they feel Congress is not doing its job.

The 95 percent rating for Harry may be one of the reasons Ralston says Harry has "a partisan attack-dog reputation"[clxxx] and why Republicans wanted

clxxviii "112th Congress: The U.S. Congress Votes Database," *The Washington Post*, January 12, 2011, http://projects.washingtonpost.com/congress/112/senate/members/.

clxxix Jonathan Allen, "112th Congress: The Worst Ever?," *Politico*, January 20, 2012, http://www.politico.com/news/stories/0112/71496.html.

clxxx Ralston, "Machiavelli with Malaprops."

Harry defeated in 2010. People from the opposing party may work especially hard to see that a majority or minority leader is defeated in the next election.

HOW LAWS ARE MADE

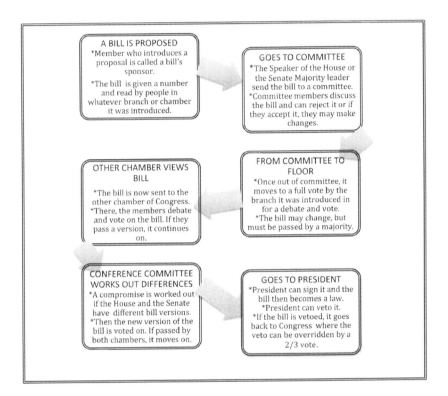

 Have you had to work on a project with someone (perhaps a classmate) whose ideas you didn't care for? How did you handle the situation? Would you handle it the same way again?

Parties once willingly compromised on issues. Why do you think the members of the two parties have had a difficult time working together in recent years? If you could advise Democrats and Republicans on how to work together, what would you suggest?

How Do Senators Help Constituents (the People They Serve)?

United States senators represent the people who elect them. They serve the needs of their states. If there is a need for a new wilderness area, for example, a U.S. senator will work to help create it. If a military base is to be shut down, the senator may work to keep it open. If a state's citizen has a specific request, one of the senators from the state will try to help. It is part of a senator's job. All senators:

- make nominations for students to attend the U.S. Naval Academy, U.S. Air Force Academy, Merchant Marine Academy, and U.S. Military Academy;
- can request that a flag be flown over the Capitol; the flag is sent to the person who requested it, and the flag's owner can proudly say his or her flag has flown over the United States Capitol;
- help small business with resources;
- provide information on internships;
- provide special recognition to people of their states;
- help set up tours of the Capitol and the White House;
- set up meetings with visitors from their respective states, if possible.[clxxxi]

Think about it! Why might you want to contact your senator someday? Would you want to tour the Capitol or the White House? In high school, would you want a nomination to one of the academies? Would you want help in setting up your own business? Or is there something else you could imagine contacting your senator about?

[clxxxi] "Harry Reid Services for Nevadans," *United States Senator for Nevada Harry Reid*, accessed December 15, 2013, http://www.reid.senate.gov/.

As a way to stay in touch with students, Senator Reid has a web page called "Youth Central Page" (http://www.reid.senate.gov/services/youthcentral). On it, he mentions what he has done specifically for the youth of Nevada. The page also links to sites that children might enjoy, such as Kids.gov (http://kids.usa.gov/), FBI kids (http://www.fbi.gov/fun-games/kids/kids), the CIA's Kids' Zone (https://www.cia.gov/kids-page), and the Nevada Department of Tourism and Cultural Affairs' Nevada Kids Page (http://www.nevadaculture.org/indexcdbf.html).

A senator tries to be available to his constituents, even those too young to vote. He answers questions from scouts, children who may have school projects, or those who are curious about some aspect of government.

What question would you want one of Nevada's senators or congressmen to answer? Is there another source where you might find the answer? It's unlikely that our busy representatives will return an answer within 24 hours, so how long would be reasonable?

How quickly do you answer emails? Get your homework done? Do your chores? How do others feel when you don't finish a task quickly?

REID'S POLITICS

R EID LIKES TO tell about his grandma, Harriet Reid. She was an independent woman. What gave her this independence? Harry believed it was the payment she received each month from the government. Known as Social Security Retirement Benefits, these payments provided the money on which she lived. She didn't need to rely on her family.[clxxxii] Not surprisingly, Harry has been a strong supporter of Social Security benefits. The Social Security Act aids widows, orphans, and the disabled. He wouldn't like to see the program become private or part of a voucher system. In a voucher system, a document guaranteeing a certain amount of money is provided to a person who qualifies. The person can use the money to pay for approved services.

At the request of Grateful Dead drummer Mickey Hart, Harry sponsored an alternative-medicine amendment to the Older Americans Act. The expense of musical therapy would be covered in rest homes for the elderly. Hart noticed how his grandmother had responded to his drumming, although she reacted to little else. A signed poster of the Grateful Dead, given as a thank you from Hart to Harry, hung in Harry's Searchlight home.[clxxxiii]

[clxxxii] Reid, *The Good Fight*, 146-147.
[clxxxiii] Nagourney, "Reid Faces Battles…"

SUCCESS FOR OTHERS

WHAT BILLS HAS Harry supported? He believes they are bills that will help others. His ideas about how to help others are in line with those of the Democratic Party.

One law that has caused him difficulty is the Affordable Care Act (ACA). Republicans fought against the bill. Harry, as majority leader, worked with President Obama to pass it. People of both parties refer to it as "Obamacare." The first part to be enacted allowed children to stay on their families' health-insurance policies until age 26, if they had no other insurance. Other parts went into effect in 2014 and 2015. As 2013 drew to a close, people were signing up for medical insurance. In 2014 and 2015, large numbers of people began taking part in Obamacare.

 Young people tend to be healthy. For Obamacare to succeed, young, healthy people need to get insurance. Why do you think that is so? Why would or wouldn't you sign up for something you might not need or want?

You are not required to buy a raffle ticket for anything. However, would you buy a raffle ticket to win a new bicycle? Why or why not? Do you think buying a raffle ticket and ACA have anything in common?

As the act is fully implemented, people will be required to have health insurance. Harry believes that, under ACA, children will receive better care from pediatricians or physicians and will have better access to dental care and vision tests.

Also, ACA provides improved funding for home-visit programs. Such programs aim to lower the numbers of deaths of babies and mothers by offering health care for expectant mothers and their unborn babies. After a mother gives birth, the newborn receives necessary care. The act provides services to improve parenting skills and develop children's readiness for school.[clxxxiv]

Harry also supported Nevada Check Up. In 2009, the program, known as CHIP, funded health care for about 22,000 children each month.

All senators voted for the Healthy and Hunger-Free Kids Act. It provides nutritious meals for children whose families cannot afford breakfast or lunch. The program encourages the use of fresh food instead of cheaper processed food. It encourages schools to buy goods produced locally. More importantly for some, the act removes junk food and soda from vending machines in schools.[clxxxv]

 Think about it! How do you feel about the changes in what vending machines offer? Michelle Obama, President Obama's wife, has taken on children's obesity as one of her causes. Are you, or do you know, someone who should make more healthy choices? What healthy choices do you try to make? How could you help a friend eat better without making him or her feel bad? Should you try to advise a friend on how to eat?

Under Harry's leadership, the Reconnecting Homeless Youth Act was passed in 2008. The law provides help for youth shelters, educational assistance, and appropriate housing for youths. The American Recovery and

---

[clxxxiv] "Children," *United States Senator for Nevada Harry Reid*, accessed July 24, 2015, http://www.reid.senate.gov/issues/children.

[clxxxv] "School Meals," *United States Department of Agriculture (USDA) Food and Nutrition Service*, last modified March 3, 2014, http://www.fns.usda.gov/school-meals/healthy-hunger-free-kids-act.

Reinvestment Act, passed in 2009, provided over a billion dollars toward preventing young people from becoming homeless.

As Harry states on his web page, he was pleased that various laws he helped pass, made it easier for low- and moderate-income Nevada students to better afford college by increasing grant money.[clxxxvi] It also allowed for a "partially refundable tax credit for tuition, fees, or textbooks."[clxxxvii]

Because of Harry's help, Nevada received almost $500 million to fund schools, colleges, and universities.[clxxxviii]

Along with a majority of senators, Harry voted for the Garrett Lee Smith Memorial Act. It provides money for three programs aimed at reducing suicide among youths.

Harry, of course, has supported hundreds of bills that he feels help the people of his state and the nation. Senators from all states do the same, but they don't agree on the best way to help.

Harry's views have caused the anger of those who don't want to see the government involved in more programs.

 If you could advise a senator or congressman from Nevada, what three items below would you rank as most important to work on? Why? What advice would you give?
- business
- crime
- education
- the environment
- gas prices
- gun safety
- immigration
- science/NASA
- unemployment
- water
- something else?

[clxxxvi] "Education," *United States Senator for Nevada Harry Reid*, October 13, 2013, http://www.reid.senate.gov/issues/education.

[clxxxvii] "Youth Central, Keeping the Door to College Open," *United States Senator for Nevada Harry Reid*, October 12, 2013, http://www.reid.senate.gov/services/youthcentral.

[clxxxviii] "Reid Secures Nearly $14 Million in Education, Labor and Health Care Funding for Nevada," Press Release, *United States Senator for Nevada Harry Reid*, July 28, 2010, http://www.reid.senate.gov/?s=%24500+million+to+fund+schools%2C+colleges&lang=en.

SOME OF HARRY'S
OTHER INTERESTS AND VIEWS

Guns: Harry's views on gun rights earned him a grade of B in 2010 by the National Rifle Association (NRA). A score of B, according to the NRA, means he is generally pro-gun but has supported some gun reforms that the NRA opposes. Harry believes Americans should be allowed to have guns. However, he favors some restrictions. In particular, he has voted to require background checks on people purchasing firearms at gun shows. Those who favor gun restrictions are unhappy with Harry's views.

As the 2013 (113th Congress) session began, legislators considered the use of assault weapons. Since a number of mass shootings that occurred in 2012 and 2013, Harry and other senators have rethought their views about whether to ban weapons that can continually fire numerous rounds before being reloaded.[clxxxix]

 Think about it! The deaths of 26 people, including 20 school children, at Sandy Hook Elementary School in Newtown, Connecticut, in December 2012 stirred up controversy about gun laws. Would you want your teacher to carry a weapon in case there was an attack at your school? Do you have suggestions for school officials on how to handle security at your school? Most schools have good security. Is your school one of those?

[clxxxix] Amanda Terkel, "Harry Reid Comes Out for Ban on Assault Weapons, High-Capacity Magazines," *Huff Post Politics*, April 17, 2013, http://www.huffingtonpost.com/2013/04/17/harry-reid-assault-weapons-ban_n_3100164.html.

Some people question whether we are a violent society. Are movies too violent? What about the cartoons you watch, or the games you play? Are there too many fights or too much screaming at sporting events? Why or why not?

Mining: In Nevada, mining is an important industry. People in this state mine for gold and silver. Harry's father was a miner, and conditions were sometimes unsafe for him and others. According to a page on Reid's website entitled "Position on the Issues," Harry has supported legislation he believes will provide a "safer, cleaner and more profitable mining industry."[cxc] The mining industry lobby is among the five largest in the country, and it dislikes some of Harry's votes on regulating the industry. Harry feels mine workers could use more protection from accidents. Mine owners feel they take proper precautions to prevent accidents. However, Harry has blocked potential updates to the General Mining Law of 1872, which allows mine owners to earn money without paying royalties to the government.[cxci]

Yucca Mountain: The two senators from Nevada often work together on issues. Both former Senator Ensign and Senator Reid were against using Yucca Mountain, near Las Vegas, as a place to store nuclear waste.

Harry and former Senator Ensign wrote a bill to protect over 444,000 acres of wilderness near Las Vegas. Harry and Senator Heller, who replaced Ensign, also work together to help Nevadans, including preventing the use of Yucca Mountain. Nevada's two senators will also disagree on many issues because they are not members of the same party and hold different views.

[cxc] "Mining," *United States Senator for Nevada Harry Reid*, accessed December 29, 2010, http://reid.senate.gov/index.cfm.

[cxci] Josh Harkinson, "Harry Reid, Gold Member," *Mother Jones*, March/April 2009, http://www.motherjones.com/environment/2009/02/harry-reid-gold-member.

Think about it! The Democratic and Republican parties differ on many issues, but they both work for the good of citizens. They have different beliefs on how this should be accomplished. Differences exist when it comes to such issues as the role of the federal government versus the role of states, certain rights of citizens, taxes, gun control, immigration, and education. You've read about Senator Reid's positions. On which do you agree? On which do you disagree?

Over the years, Harry's views have changed. One *New York Times* writer says, "Washington has observed in Mr. Reid an evolution—less flip-flops than slow dances to the left—that reflect shifting attitudes not only in the Democratic conference, but also in Nevada. . . ."[cxcii]

Typical Democratic and Republican Ideologies or Views on Some Issues

Issue	Many Democrats believe in...	Many Republicans believe in...
Progress vs. Tradition	social progress and change	traditional values—keeping things as they are
Individualism	government of, for, and by the people	honoring individual achievement
The Constitution	an interpretation that changes with the times	a strict interpretation, along lines of the Founding Fathers
The Economy	higher tax rates for the richest Americans	reducing taxes for all
Minimum Wage	a higher minimum wage	wages that reflect the economy
The Military	decreased spending	increased spending
Abortion	the right of a woman to make her own decision (for abortion rights)	no abortions, though under special circumstances some will make exceptions
Gun Control	restrictions on the sale of certain types of guns and a waiting period before being able to purchase a weapon	no restrictions at gun shows and no waiting periods (the NRA's position on gun control)

[cxcii] Steinhauer, "As Views Shift on Guns…"

Role of Government	a strong central government that can make policy and allow for more equal practices across the nation	power held more closely to the people, meaning on the state or local level
Education	strong support for public schools	school choice through vouchers
Immigration	help for illegal immigrant children whose parents brought them to the U.S. at a young age	no help to children of illegal immigrants
Health Care	full enforcement of the Affordable Health Care Act	no enforcement of the Affordable Health Care Act
Environment	government protecting the environment through laws	individuals (and companies) protecting the environment because they have an interest in doing so
General Philosophy	social action programs and a greater role for government in society	individuals being responsible for their own successes

Find out more about the issues. Read both sides of an issue to make an intelligent decision. Each party tends to clearly present information in favor of its viewpoint. Good citizens learn the facts and try to understand how a position may turn out.

Though Harry is a Mormon, his views aren't the same as those of most Mormons. Harry holds the highest position in the United States government of any other LDS church member. However, some in that community have questioned how well Harry follows the church's teachings. Because the church tends to support Republican views, Harry's ideas are in the minority. Only 17 percent of Mormons are Democrats or prefer Democratic Party views.[cxciii] However, Harry feels his Democratic Party positions are in line with the LDS faith because Mormons believe in helping the poor and taking care of the land. In eight states, not including Nevada, Mormons who identified themselves as Democrats formed a national organization in 2013 to share their religious and political beliefs.[cxciv] In January 2013, during the 113th

[cxciii] Brian Passey, "Mormon Liberals: A 'Minority Within a Minority,'" *USA Today*, October 30, 2012, http://www.usatoday.com/story/news/politics/2012/10/30/mormon-liberals-minority/1669155/.

[cxciv] Lisa Riley Roche, "Mormon Democrats Announce New National State Organizations," *Deseret News*, April 4, 2013, http://www.deseretnews.com/article/865577470/Mormon-Democrats-announce-new-national-state-organizations.html?pg=all.

Congress, seven Senate members identified themselves as Mormons. Of those, five were Republicans and two, including Harry, were Democrats. In the House of Representatives, three are Democrats and ten are Republicans.[cxcv]

No matter the leanings of LDS church members, the church itself cannot officially support Democratic or Republican candidates. Any church, temple, or mosque that supports a candidate would lose its tax-free status as a religious organization.

 How much do your religious beliefs influence your views? Is that sometimes a problem?

[cxcv] "Mormons in Congress 2012 – Final Results," *By Common Consent*, November 9, 2012, http://bycommon-consent.com/2012/11/09/mormons-in-congress-2012-final-results-2/.

OUR WORDS ARE IMPORTANT

MANY PEOPLE HAVE been upset by some of Harry's words. He has said, "I speak bluntly. Sometimes I can be impulsive . . . This has not always necessarily served me well. . . ."[cxcvi] Over the years, Harry has made statements that others, especially his opponents, have pounced upon. Below are some of the most quoted ones:

- "Obama was more electable because he's 'light-skinned' and lacked a 'Negro dialect,' unless he wanted to have one." Not only was the use of "Negro" outdated, but the comment that light-skinned African-Americans have a better chance of success is viewed as racist.

- "My staff tells me not to say this, but I'm going to say it anyway. In the summer, because of the heat and high humidity, you could literally smell the tourists coming into the Capitol. It may be descriptive but it's true." Harry said this just after the $621 million U.S. Capitol Visitor Center was completed.

- On the Iraq war: "This war is lost." At the time this statement was made in April 2007, violence in Iraq was especially bad. Many felt Harry should have made a statement supporting American forces.

---

cxcvi Reid, *The Good Fight*, 20-21.

- On the death of Senator Ted Kennedy (D-Mass.) in August 2009: "I think it's going to help us." Harry was referring to the fact that Kennedy's death might encourage people to vote for the Affordable Care Act in memory of Kennedy. This remark was viewed as insensitive.

- On President George W. Bush in May 2005: "I think this guy is a loser." Harry said he has apologized for that line. He also called Bush a "liar" but would not apologize for that word.

- To a *Las Vegas Review-Journal* executive in August 2009: "I hope you go out of business." Harry had been attacked by a reporter at the *Review-Journal*. Harry claimed his sense of humor was being misunderstood.

- In July 2012, Harry caused a huge stir by saying that Mitt Romney, the Republican presidential candidate, had not paid any taxes in the last ten years. Romney and fellow Republicans wanted Harry to prove his statement. Others felt it was up to Romney to prove him wrong. As the election ended, Harry had offered neither an apology nor any proof about the tax issue. After President Obama was re-elected, people were no longer interested in Romney's tax returns. Harry knew that what he had said was dirty politics.[cxcvii]

Think about it!

Do you think Senator Reid should have apologized for any of the above quotes? If so, which?

Many people, including presidents, senators, congressmen, and candidates for office, make foolish comments. How should inappropriate comments be handled?

What happens when you say something you shouldn't have? Is it possible to take back your words? What if a statement is true but hurtful? Should you still make it?

[cxcvii] Sam Stein, "The Remarkable and Complex Legacy of One Harry Reid," *The Huffington Post*, March 27, 2015, http://www.huffingtonpost.com/2015/03/27/harry-reid-retires_n_6957414.html.

Harry has also misvoted twice on an important bill. On Christmas Eve 2009, he voted against the health-care bill he had been trying so hard to get passed. His error was caused by tiredness.[cxcviii] In March, he again made the same mistake.[cxcix]

[cxcviii] Nagourney, "Reid Faces Battles…"
[cxcix] Jeremy W. Peters, "In Landmark Vote, Senate Limits Use of the Filibuster," *The New York Times*, November 21, 2013, http://www.nytimes.com/2013/11/22/us/politics/reid-sets-in-motion-steps-to-limit-use-of-fili-buster.html?_r=0.

OUT TO GET HIM

A S THE 2010 congressional races geared up, Harry Reid ran for his
fifth term. Some people had cited the 2009–2010 Congress as the most
productive since the 1960s.[cc] However, it was successful for the Democratic
agenda under Majority Leader Reid. So Harry was the candidate Republicans most wanted to defeat. It looked as if Republicans would succeed.
Money poured into Nevada to defeat Harry. Negative ads by both Harry
and his opponent filled the airwaves. Polls predicted a close race and a
possible loss for Harry.

Sharron Angle, a Tea Party candidate, won the Republican State Primary. She would run against Harry. Not all Republicans were happy with
her selection.

Tea Party

Since 2009, the Tea Party has been active. Its members believe
in a strict interpretation of the Constitution, reducing government
spending, keeping taxes low for all Americans, and reducing the
national debt.

Members of the Tea Party have voted overwhelmingly with
Republicans.

[cc] George Zornick, "111th Congress Was Most Productive Session Since 'At Least' the 1960s," *Think Progress,* December 23, 2010, http://thinkprogress.org/politics/2010/12/23/136353/111-congress-achievement/.

> The name comes from the Boston Tea Party, which took place on December 16, 1773. American patriots refused to pay the taxes the British imposed on tea and other imported items. "No taxation without Representation" was a refrain heard at the time. Since the British refused to send the tea back to England, some colonists boarded the boats and threw the tea overboard.

Harry started his campaign quickly. Angle needed more time to organize her campaign, since her primary win had been a surprise.

Republicans attacked Harry in every way they could. They questioned how he had become a millionaire. He had been in public life for most of his career. Harry has said he earned a lot of money as a lawyer and entered Congress as a millionaire. He invested in Nevada real estate at a time when the state was growing. A least one of his real-estate deals involving the development of a bridge between Arizona and Nevada has gotten him into trouble; the bridge would make his own land more valuable.

His enemies claimed he was among the most liberal senators. Some consider liberal policies bad for the country. Liberals tend to prefer programs run by the federal government, not the state governments. The various attacks by Republicans have been leveled against him, even when he has not been campaigning for re-election.

Republicans wanted him out of power because they felt he had become too partisan. Harry didn't allow votes to come before the Senate on some controversial issues. He was protecting Democratic senators who were up for re-election. If there were no recorded votes on an issue, the senator couldn't be attacked on that issue during a campaign. Republicans attacked Harry for not allowing votes on issues they felt were bipartisan,[cci] or favored by both parties.

[cci] Ben White, "Who'll Take the Reins from Harry Reid?," *CNBC*, March 27, 2015, http://www.cnbc.com/2015/03/27/wholl-take-the-reins-from-harry-reid.html.

With all the negative ads against him, why would he even seek office? When questioned about this at a rally on the University of Nevada, Reno campus, Harry responded, "I do it for the children."

 What do you think Harry means when he says, "I do it for the children"? What children does he mean? What is he doing? Does his record support his statement? Why or why not?

Combined, the cost of the Harry Reid's and Sharron Angle's campaigns was at least $44 million.

Harry won by 5.5 percentage points.

After the election, another scandal arose for Harry. One of the contributors to his campaign, Harvey Whittemore, was found guilty of making illegal election contributions. Harry has been suspected of helping his friend overcome problems in building a golf course.[ccii] Harry's enemies were convinced of illegal happenings. However, as of early 2015, he hasn't been implicated in any wrong dealings on the matter.

 Do you think people in political office take advantage of their jobs? Why or why not? Is it likely that people in power are examined more closely than the general population?

Since late 2012, four members of Congress have been found guilty of crimes. In almost 25 years, 15 governors have also been convicted. None have been from Nevada. Is that because Nevada's elected officials are better or luckier?

[ccii] Martha Bellisle, "Update: Feds Say Harvey Whittemore Made Illegal Donations to Gain Favor with Harry Reid," *Reno-Gazette Journal*, September 24, 2013, http://archive.rgj.com/article/20130924/NEWS/309240050/ Update-Feds-say-Harvey-Whittemore-made-illegal-donations-gain-favor-Harry-Reid.

Negative remarks are constantly hurled against Harry. In general, though, he has received praise for leading the Senate in 2013 to eliminate the so-called nuclear option. Though it sounds horrible, the nuclear option is only a type of voting procedure. With the majority needing 60 votes in order to pass legislation (called a supermajority), the minority party had been able to block the approval of some presidential nominations.

"The Senate is a living thing, and to survive it must change as it has over the history of this great country,"[cciii] Harry said. When he felt enough democratic senators would agree, Harry introduced a rule that lowered the number needed to end debate to 50. He felt, "To the average American, adapting the rules to make the Senate work again is just common sense."[cciv] Now a simple majority of 50 (not a supermajority of 60) is enough to approve many nominations. Republicans warned that once they were in the majority, Democrats would regret the change.[ccv]

Filibusters

Senators have the ability to filibuster bills to delay a vote. A filibuster occurs when a legislator makes a long speech that prevents anything else from happening in the legislature. By doing this, Congress is prevented from doing its work. The filibuster ends when the speaker leaves the podium or when there are enough votes to stop the speaker. Until 2013, a supermajority was needed to stop a filibuster.

Filibusters have long been part of our history. In 1917, many in the country wanted the U.S. to enter WWI. By using the filibuster, a small group of senators prevented a vote to declare war. President Woodrow Wilson was furious: "The Senate of the United States is the only legislative body in the world which cannot act when its majority is ready for action," he said, adding,

---

[cciii] Peters, "In Landmark Vote…"
[cciv] Ibid.
[ccv] Ibid.

"A little group of willful men, representing no opinion but their own, have rendered the great government of the United States helpless and contemptible."[ccvi]

The Senate, he demanded, must adopt a "cloture rule," which is a rule that places a closure or limitation on legislative debate. The Senate did so by agreeing to a cloture rule of two-thirds, called a supermajority, which would be needed for a measure to pass. In practice, debates could still go on for days. Achieving a two-thirds vote to close debate is very difficult and has occurred only a handful of times.[ccvii]

In 1975, a change to the rule was made so that three-fifths, or 60 senators, would be needed to prevent a filibuster.[ccviii]

Also, as Congress left for its break in 2014, it had agreed on a budget plan for the first time since 1986. So there will not be another government shutdown or threat of one for at least two years.[ccix]

[ccvi] John Milton Cooper, Jr., "Wilson, the Senate and Cloture," *The New York Times*, December 18, 2013, http://www.nytimes.com/roomfordebate/2013/12/18/the-history-and-lessons-of-congressional-crises/wilson-the-senate-and-cloture.

[ccvii] United States Senate, "March 8, 1917 Cloture Rule," *Senate History*, 1878-1920, accessed June 16, 2015, http://www.senate.gov/artandhistory/history/minute/Cloture_Rule.htm.

[ccviii] Andrew Glass, "The Senate Revises Its Cloture rule, March 7, 1975," *Politico*, March 7, 2012, http://www.politico.com/news/stories/0312/73695.html.

[ccix] Erin Kelly, "Analysts: 'Nuclear option' Likely Won't Hurt Reid," *Reno-Gazette-Journal*, November 22, 2013, 3A.

THEN CAME THE ELECTION OF 2014:
DID THEY GET HIM?

H ARRY WASN'T EVEN a candidate in the November 2014 election. Yet the election reduced his power.

Enough Republicans won Senate seats in that election that the 114th Congress, which began in January of 2015, had a Republican majority. Republican Mitch McConnell became the majority leader, making Harry the minority leader. In this role, he would no longer select the chairs of the committees nor decide on the Senate's agenda; these would now be the responsibility of the Republican majority leader.

Does this make powerful senator Harry Reid a has-been?

According to Bill Theobald, a writer with *USA Today*, when Harry was minority leader, he was "plain-talking, pugnacious and politically astute."[ccx] And he remained that way as majority leader. So there is no reason to expect him to change.

Many who follow politics said they believed Harry would be a powerful person in the 114th Congress. Eric Herzik, a professor at the University of Nevada, Reno, said that he believed Harry was practical and would work out deals to get bills passed.[ccxi] Fred Lokken from Truckee Meadows Community College said, "He still has a lot of seniority. He has a lot of IOUs

---

[ccx] Bill Theobald, "Reid Still A Force," *USA Today*, Reprinted in *Reno-Gazette Journal*, November 16, 2014, http://www.centralohio.com/usatoday/article/18548769.

[ccxi] Ibid.

that he can call up as an individual senator if he needed to."[ccxii] (An IOU is a favor that is owed someone.)

The editors of the Reno Gazette Journal have said of Harry, "there is no one more skillful in the hallways and backrooms of Congress where most of the work gets done."[ccxiii]

As a young man, Harry changed his plans to achieve his goals; as majority leader, he used similar tactics. How would Harry handle the change to his status? If the past were any indication, he would find ways to survive.

Figures 41-47: Various pictures of Harry Reid throughout his career.

[ccxii] Ibid.
[ccxiii] Nagourney, "Reid Faces Battles…"

Figure 48: Senator Reid, at his Thursday Breakfast with the public.

Figure 49: "Senator Harry Reid meets with Julian Castro, nominee for Secretary of Housing and Urban Development, in July 2014."

Figure 50: "President Barack Obama talks with Senator Reid while on Air Force One."

HEALTH ISSUES

IN GENERAL, HARRY'S health has been good.

However, in 2005, he had what his doctor called "a warning stroke." Landra heard a thump and came running. She found her husband on the floor next to the bed and called the doctor. After examining Harry, the doctor said he believed everything was fine. However, his doctor suggested a more thorough exam. When he returned to D.C. from Searchlight, Harry saw a specialist. The doctor prescribed a heart monitor for Harry to wear. The monitor revealed an irregular heartbeat. The doctor prescribed medicine, and Harry has been fine since.[ccxiv]

Landra has had a few difficult years. In March 2010, she was badly injured in a car accident, just as her husband's senatorial campaign began. Their daughter was also in the car, though she escaped injury. Landra, whose car was rear-ended by a tractor-trailer, suffered a broken neck, back, and nose. After surgery, she had a slow recovery.

In September 2011, Landra, described by Harry as the love of his life, was diagnosed with Stage 2 breast cancer. Fortunately, it was detected early; with chemotherapy, followed by radiation, her prognosis was good.

[ccxiv] Reid, The Good Fight, 207-209.

Figure 51: Landra Reid.

Cancer Stages

Though women are more likely to get breast cancer, men can, too.

Women should check with their doctors about how to do self-exams, when to have screenings (mammograms), and other ways to protect themselves.

Cancers are classified into four stages, which are determined based on the size of a tumor and whether it has spread. Stages 1 and 2 are generally considered treatable. Stages 3 and 4 are more difficult to treat.

Early detection and treatment, usually involving chemotherapy, has reduced the number of deaths from breast cancer.[ccxv]

Harry's motorcade was involved in an accident in October 2012. Because he wore a seat belt, he suffered only minor bruises. He was checked by doctors in a local Las Vegas hospital and released.[ccxvi]

In December 2013, Harry checked himself into a D.C. hospital. He had not been feeling well. Tests indicated he was suffering from exhaustion. By evening, he was home with Landra.

[ccxv] "Breast Cancer Stages," *National Breast Cancer Foundation, Inc.*, accessed May 20, 2015, http://www.nationalbreastcancer.org/breast-cancer-stages.
[ccxvi] Michelle Rindels, "Reid Leaves Hospital after Vegas Car Crash," *Associated Press*, October 26, 2012, http://www.bigstory.ap.org/article/sen-reid-taken-hospital-after-vegas-car-crash.

Then, just before the 114th Congress began, doctors ordered Harry to do his work from his Washington apartment. He had been exercising at his new home in Henderson, Nevada, on January 1, 2015, using exercise bands, which, along with 250 sit-ups, are part of his regular exercise routine. On this New Year's Day, one of his exercise bands broke. Senator Dick Durban, who visited him, said, "Reid was stretching these straps and one broke and tossed him like a slingshot against built-in cabinets. He crashed into them with his face and side of his body. . . ."[ccxvii] Harry's right eye was blackened, and he didn't know whether he would lose sight in the eye. In addition, he broke three ribs and some facial bones, and was bruised in other places.[ccxviii]

Only time will tell what long-term physical effects his injuries will have. Since he hurt himself, Harry has had two surgeries. The first, which took three and a half hours, was to remove a blood clot.[ccxix] The second surgery repaired the broken bones. At the time of this writing, as he recovers, Harry continues to exercise, but not with the bands that caused the injury. For an hour each day, he walks around the basketball court in his building. He claims he won't be using the exercise bands anymore.

In an interview that he gave on April 8, 2015, Harry said of his right eye, "I can't see out of my eye, and that's the way it's going to be until something comes along that'll change it."[ccxx]

The right side of his face was still bruised three months after the accident, but the senator was back at work nonetheless.

[ccxvii] Andrew Taylor, "Injuries Force Reid to Skip Opening Session of Senate," *The Washington Times*, January 6, 2015, http://www.washingtontimes.com/news/2015/jan/6/injuries-force-reid-to-skip-opening-session-of-sen/.

[ccxviii] Ed O'Keefe, "Harry Reid Describes Exercise Injuries, Doesn't Rule Out Losing Sight in His Right Eye," *The Washington Post*, January 9, 2015, http://www.washingtonpost.com/blogs/post-politics/wp/2015/01/09/harry-reid-describes-exercise-injuries-doesnt-rule-out-losing-sight-in-his-right-eye/.

[ccxix] Alan Rappeport, "Reid is Home After Surgery for Injuries," January 26, 2015, *The New York Times*, http://www.nytimes.com/2015/01/27/us/politics/reid-is-home-after-surgery-for-injuries.html?ref=topics&_r=0.

[ccxx] Rebecca Kaplan, "Harry Reid Has Lost His Vision in His Right Eye," *CBS News*, April 8, 2015, http://www.cbsnews.com/news/harry-reid-has-lost-his-vision-in-his-right-eye/.

LANDRA, HARRY, AND FAMILY

L ANDRA HAS BEEN at Harry's side since high school. Family has always been important to them.

Together, they have raised five children, though Harry gives Landra credit for that. In *The Good Fight*, Harry writes that the family usually had dinner together when the children were young. Often, he could be found at the children's ball games. Without fail, on Sundays, the Reid family would attend church together. Each of their children graduated from Brigham Young University, a school associated with the Mormon Church. Harry and Landra are proud of their children and what they have achieved.[ccxxi] By moving to Las Vegas in 2014, the Reids would be closer to their children and grandchildren. Also, Harry would save travel time to D.C.

Figure 52: "Harry and Landra Reid with their four sons and daughter."

[ccxxi] Reid, *The Good Fight*, 279.

Harry and Landra have led a quiet life. The couple rarely attends dinner parties in Washington. Harry likes to do yoga with Landra, run, read, see movies, and watch the Washington Nationals play baseball. They seem to have a close relationship.

A SURPRISE?

PEOPLE SPECULATED AS to whether Harry would run again in 2016. Would it be good for Nevada to lose Harry, one of the most powerful people in the Senate? Many in Nevada don't like him, while, of course, there are many others who feel he has been good for Nevada.

Harry is among the most senior Senators; only five have served longer. On January 3, 2013, Harry became the "longest-serving member of Congress in Nevada history."[ccxxii]

Now that he was 75, how long would he want to continue putting in the long hours required of a senator? As of this writing, he continues to receive death threats—especially from people who oppose his views on immigration. For how long would he want to continue living under constant threats?

At first, Harry said he would run again in 2016. Rumors suggested that Brian Sandoval, the governor of Nevada at the time, might seek Harry's seat. However, rumors aren't always based in truth.

 Think about it! How do you think campaigns should be run? Should a candidate run negative ads against his opponent? Is it okay to use an opponent's words against him? Campaign experts feel negative ads work. What do you think?

[ccxxii] Erin Kelly, "Record Set for Longevity of Service," *Reno Gazette-Journal*, January 3, 2013, 3A.

Should money be allowed to pour into the state from else-where? How does money affect races? What is your idea of how a campaign should be run? How early should it start?

How would you handle running for a school office?

Political analyst Jon Ralston summarized Harry's ability to win elections in his headline, "Harry Reid's Down, But Never Out." However, Ralston did wonder whether Harry would run again in 2016.[ccxxiii]

On March 27, 2015, came an announcement that surprised many. Harry Reid said he would not run for re-election.

Harry gave several reasons. "I have had time to ponder and to think. We've got to be more concerned about the country, the Senate, the state of Nevada than about ourselves."[ccxxiv] Harry said he wanted the Democrats to become the majority party once again. He felt, "it is inappropriate for me to soak up all those resources on me when I could be devoting those resources to the caucus, and that's what I intend to do."[ccxxv]

"I want to be able to go out at the top of my game," Harry said.[ccxxvi] "I want to be able to be somebody that starts the game every day and can play." He feared his "legacy would be tarnished."[ccxxvii]

He claimed this wasn't about his health nor the tough re-election he would likely face.[ccxxviii]

Kind words poured in, especially from Democrats. President Obama said, "Above all else, Harry has fought for the people of his beloved state of

[ccxxiii] Jon Ralston, "Harry Reid's Down, But Never Out," *Politico*, February 17, 2015, http://www.politico.com/magazine/story/2015/02/harry-reid-2016-jon-ralston-115234.html#.

[ccxxiv] "What Harry Reid Said – and Reactions from Around the U.S.," *Reno-Gazette-Journal*, March 27, 2015, http://www.rgj.com/story/news/2015/03/27/what-harry-reid-said-and-reactions/70537576/.

[ccxxv] Ibid.

[ccxxvi] Hulse, "Harry Reid to Retire from Senate in 2016."

[ccxxvii] Paul Kane, "Harry Reid to Lay Aside Gloves, Retire from Senate," *The Washington Post*, March 27, 2015, http://www.washingtonpost.com/politics/harry-reid-to-lay-aside-gloves-retire-from-senate/2015/03/27/07437f6e-d4c1-11e4-a62f-ee745911a4ff_story.html.

[ccxxviii] Kane, "Harry Reid to Lay Aside Gloves…"

Nevada . . . he never stopped working to give everyone who works hard the same shot at success that he had."[ccxxix]

In a statement, Governor Sandoval of Nevada said, "Senator Reid's story is one that represents the Nevada and American dream . . . Senator Reid has been an influential voice in Congress on behalf of Nevada's interests." Sandoval went on to list some of Harry Reid's achievements.[ccxxx]

The Nevada Democratic Party called Harry "the most effective fighter the state of Nevada has ever had in the United States Senate."[ccxxxi]

According to CNBC, "Republicans, who loathe Harry with an unrestrained passion, celebrated the news."[ccxxxii]

[ccxxix] "What Harry Reid Said…"
[ccxxx] Ibid.
[ccxxxi] Ibid.
[ccxxxii] White, "Who'll Take the Reins from Harry Reid?"

THE AMERICAN DREAM?

ARRY IS THE most successful politician to emerge from Nevada. He has also held the highest office in the country of any member of the LDS church.

He is important enough to have been evacuated from D.C. by a military helicopter on 9/11. He and other top officials were taken to an undisclosed "safe place" in Virginia.

He is important enough to have a spacious office in the Russell Senate Building. Senators have two offices in D.C.—one in the Hart Building and one in the Russell Senate Building. The Russell Building is adjacent to the Senate, and most offices there are small. They usually each contain a cot, sink, and toilet. Harry, as one of the Senate's leaders, has a large office in which to meet people and conduct business.

Sam Stein of *The Huffington Post* called Reid "one of the greatest tacticians in modern Senate history, someone who combined a mastery of the rules and a keen recognition of the country's ideological drift." [ccxxxiii] Stein also referred to Reid as one of the most influential political figures of the past six years, second only to President Barack Obama. [ccxxxiv] And to think, he grew up in a town that could only provide an eighth-grade education to its children.

[ccxxxiii] Stein, "The Remarkable and Complex Legacy..."
[ccxxxiv] Ibid.

Harry Reid no longer needs to chase jackrabbits for his next meal. If anything, his concern is more with which restaurant to choose. Harry doesn't need to worry about how he will pay his bills, including his wife's large medical bills. He, like all members of Congress, has a comfortable income and health insurance. He has money in the bank. By many measures, he has been very successful.

Part of the reason for his success is that Harry's a fighter. Many problems could have ended his quest for success. But he never gave up.

Harry also succeeded because he was fortunate to have had people like Mike O'Callaghan to mentor him. Harry succeeded because of the support he received from his family, especially Landra.

Harry succeeded because he has an education.

Harry succeeded because he worked hard.

On November 17, 2004, Harry told an interviewer on FOX television, "If I can make it in America anyone can."

He knows his story is a miracle.[ccxxxv]

Harry lives the American Dream. Not bad for a poor boy from Searchlight. Somebody forgot to tell him he was supposed to be "a nobody."

 Can you create your own luck? Who can you get to mentor you? How hard are you willing to work to achieve your dreams?

[ccxxxv] "What Harry Reid Said..."

GOVERNMENT TERMS USED
IN SOMEBODY FORGOT TO TELL HARRY

Amendment: a change or addition to the Constitution. The fifth Article of the United States Constitution sets forth the process for making changes. The first ten are known as The Bill of Rights.

American Dream: the belief that the United States is a land of opportunity and that anyone who works hard can be successful.

Antifederalists: people who opposed ratifying the U. S. Constitution because it proposed a strong central government.

Articles of Confederation: drawn up in 1776-1777, the first constitution of the United States. It went into effect in 1781; its contents prevented a weak national government from working well.

Bill of Rights: the first ten amendments to the Constitution; became part of the Constitution in1791 and provide specific rights to American citizens, such as the right to free speech and freedom of the press.

Caucus: a gathering of party members to make decisions, such as which candidate to nominate for an office, what policies to set, and what strategies to follow.

Census: an official count of the population performed every ten years. Used to decide number of members in the House of Representatives.

Cloture: a procedure for ending debate in the legislature, usually by calling a vote; number of votes needed for cloture has changed over the years.

Connecticut Compromise: also called the Great Compromise. Resulted in the two houses of the United States Congress. The House of Representatives, or lower house, selects its members based on each state's population. The Senate, or upper house, has two members from each state.

Congress: the legislature; the part of government that makes laws. The United States has two houses in its legislature: the Senate and the House of Representatives.

Constituents: the voters in a district or state who elect a representative to serve in Congress.

Constitutional Convention: held in Philadelphia in 1787, and called to make changes to the Articles of Confederation: this first constitution was not working. The basis for the constitution which governs the United States today.

Democratic Party: one of two major parties in the United States. Known for supporting minorities, labor unions, and ideas reflecting reform.

Enact: to pass a bill into law.

Entitlements: government programs that provide benefits to a certain group, such as the unemployed or the disabled.

Equal Rights Amendment: proposed amendment that would end discrimination against women; it failed to be ratified.

Extradition: a legal process that moves an alleged criminal from one state to another where the crime was supposed to have been committed or where the trial will take place.

Federalists: supporters of the Constitution, written in 1787, felt a strong central government was needed. Also the name of an early political party that lasted from 1789 to 1801 and favored a strong central government.

Filibuster: a speech used to slow down or prevent a vote in the legislature, usually in the Senate, on a controversial issue.

Grandfather clause: the way in which several U.S. states allowed only white voters to cast ballots. A person could vote if his grandfather was eligible to vote before 1867. It kept blacks from voting, since their grandfathers had been slaves.

Great Compromise: see Connecticut Compromise.

Gun control: a movement in the United States aimed at restricting the sale and use of firearms.

Ideology: a set of beliefs held by a person that influences the way he or she behaves and sees the world. Guides a person's political, religious, or economic actions.

Incumbent: the person holding an elected office.

Independent: a person who is not a member of a political party.

Legislature: the group with the power to create laws.

Legislation: the laws or measures enacted by the legislature.

Lobbying: the attempt to influence the decisions made by public officials, especially legislators.

Lobbyist: a person trying to influence members of Congress.

Majority leader: the leader selected by the political party that holds the majority in the legislature.

Majority rule: the concept that fifty percent plus one or more of a group has the power to make decisions for which the entire group follows.

Nineteenth Amendment: passed in 1920, gave women the right to vote.

Political parties: organizations that seek power by electing people to office so that their positions become the policies of the country.

Primaries: elections in which voters choose candidates to run for office.

Republican Party: one of two major parties in the United States. Known for supporting minimal government regulations, lower taxes, and traditional values.

Seniority: the status obtained by the length of service a person has in Congress.

Separation of Powers: a constitutional division of powers among the legislative, executive, and judicial branches, with the legislative branch making law, the executive applying and enforcing the law, and the judiciary interpreting the law.

Social Security: a U.S. government insurance plan begun in 1935 in which the employer and employee contribute money. Pays for retirement benefits, health insurance for the elderly, and support for disabled workers and the children of deceased or disabled workers.

Tea Party: a political party that opposes high taxation, immigration, and government interference in the people's lives.

Voucher: a form or check giving credit for future expenses. In the case of "school vouchers," for example, the government provides monetary help to parents who wish their children to attend private, rather than public, schools.

Whip: a party leader whose job it is to encourage its members to vote a certain way on bills.

SOURCES:

"Britannica Kids," *Encyclopaedia Britannica Kids*, accessed June 4, 2015, http://kids.britannica.com/.

"Congressional Glossary – Including Legislative and Budget Terms (CongressionalGlossary.com), *Hobnob Blog*, accessed August 6, 2015, http://hobnobblog.com/congressional-glossary-including-legislative-and-budget-terms/

The Dirkson Congressional Center, "Legislative Branch," *Congress for Kids*, accessed August 6, 2015, http://congressforkids.net/Legislative-branch_senate.htm.

BIBLIOGRAPHY

"112th Congress: The U.S. Congress Votes Database." *The Washington Post*, January 12, 2011. http://projects.washingtonpost.com/congress/112/senate/members/.

"1960's Food and Groceries Prices." *The People History*. Accessed July 7, 2013. http://www.thepeoplehistory.com/60sfood.html.

"About Senator Harry Reid." *United States Senator for Nevada Harry Reid*. Accessed November 10, 2014. http://www.reid.senate.gov/about.

"About – Yosemite 125th Anniversary/NPS." *National Park Service*. Accessed May 20, 2015. http://www.nps.gov/featurecontent/yose/anniversary/about/index.html.

Abraham, David K. "A Brief History of the American Two Party System." Accessed May 20, 2015. http://davidkabraham.com/OldWeb/Beliefs/America/twopartysystem.htm.

Adams, Mark. "The Forum That Foreshadows: Notable Alumni from the Sun Youth Forum." *Las Vegas Weekly*, November 13, 2013. http://www.lasvegasweekly.com/as-we-see-it/2013/nov/13/notable-alumni-sun-youth-forum/.

Allen, Jonathan. "112th Congress: The Worst Ever?" *Politico*, January 20, 2012. http://www.politico.com/news/stories/0112/71496.html.

Batt, Marissa N. "Just Verdicts." *Ms. Magazine*, Summer 2004. Accessed June 16, 2015. http://www.msmagazine.com/summer2004/justverdicts. asp.

Begala, Paul. "Harry Reid: King of the Hill." *CNN*, October 17, 2013. http://www.cnn.com/2013/10/17/opinion/begala-shutdown-showdown.

Bellisle, Martha. "Update: Feds Say Harvey Whittemore Made Illegal Donations to Gain Favor with Harry Reid." *Reno-Gazette Journal*, September 24, 2013. http://archive.rgj.com/article/20130924/NEWS/309240050/Update-Feds-say-Harvey-Whittemore-made-illegal-donations-gain-favor-Harry-Reid.

Borrell, Brendon. "What is Truth Serum? *Scientific American*, December 4, 2008. http://www.scientificamerican.com/article/what-is-truth-serum/.

"Breast Cancer Stages." *National Breast Cancer Foundation, Inc.* Accessed May 20, 2015. http://www.nationalbreastcancer.org/breast-cancer-stages.

"Bristlecone Pines." Great Basin National Park Nevada. *National Park Service*. Last modified July 24, 2015. http://www.nps.gov/grba/planyourvisit/identifying-bristlecone-pines.htm.

Brown, Sandra. "America the Beautiful: A History of the Right to Vote in the US." *League of Women Voters, Albuquerque-Bernalillo County*. Last modified April 7, 2005. http://www.lwvabc.org/pubs/history_of_vote.html.

"Children." *United States Senator for Nevada Harry Reid*. Accessed July 24, 2015. http://www.reid.senate.gov/issues/children.

Cooper, John Milton, Jr. "Wilson, the Senate and Cloture." *The New York Times*, December 18, 2013. http://www.nytimes.com/roomfordebate/2013/12/18/the-history-and-lessons-of-congressional-crises/wilson-the-senate-and-cloture.

Cooper, Rachel. "What is a Lobbyist? FAQs About Lobbying." *About Travel.* Accessed July 10, 2015. http://dc.about.com/od/jobs/a/Lobbying.htm.

DeAngelis, Gina. *Jackie Robinson.* New York: Chelsea House, November 2000.

"Definition." *Domestic Violence Handbook.* Last modified January 5, 2015. www.domesticviolence.org/definition/.

DiBella, Suzan. "Connected at the Roots." *UNLV Magazine*, Fall 2004. Accessed December 9, 2014. http://news.unlv.edu/unlvmagazineIssues/Fall04/reid.html.

Diseases and Conditions Rheumatic Fever." *Mayo Clinic.* Accessed April 21, 2015. http://www.mayoclinic.org/diseases-conditions/rheumatic-fever/basics/causes/con-20031399.

"Education." *United States Senator for Nevada Harry Reid.* Last modified October 13, 2013. http://www.reid.senate.gov/issues/education.

Elliott, Stephen. "Searching for Harry Reid." *The Progressive*, March 2005. http://www.progressive.org/news/2006/11/4202/searching-harry- reid.

"El Rey-2012." *Queho Posse.* Accessed July 26, 2015, http://www.quehoposse.org/index.php/plaques/43-el-rey.

"Epilepsy: Fact Sheet." *World Health Organization.* Accessed May, 2015, http://www.who.int/mediacentre/factsheets/fs999/en/.

"Epilepsy Stats and Facts." *Epilepsy Foundation.* Accessed April 22, 2015, http://www.epilepsy.com/connect/forums/living-epilepsy-adults/epilepsy-stats-and-facts.

Evans, K.J. "Harry Reid." *Las Vegas Review Journal*, September 12, 1999. http://www.reviewjournal.com/news/harry-reid. "Facts and Statistics." *Church of Jesus Christ of Latter-Day Saints Newsroom.* Last modified February 21, 2012. http://www.mormonnewsroom.org/facts-and-statistics/country/united-states/.

"Famous People with Epilepsy." *Disabled World*. Accessed April 22, 2015. http://www.disabled-world.com/artman/publish/epilepsy-famous.shtml.

"Gaming Commission." *Nevada Gaming Control Board*. Accessed June 16, 2015. http://gaming.nv.gov/index.aspx?page=3.

Glass, Andrew. "The Senate Revises Its Cloture Rule, March 7, 1975." *Politico*, March 7, 2012. http://www.politico.com/news/stories/0312/ 73695. html.

Gutenberg, Virginia. Telephone interview, March 3, 2015.

Harkinson, Josh. "Harry Reid, Gold Member." *Mother Jones*, March/April 2009, http://www.motherjones.com/environment/2009/02/harry-re-id-gold-member.

"Harry Reid." *Internet Movie Database*. Accessed April 27, 2015. http://www.imdb.com/name/nm0717285/.

History Channel. "Korean War." *A&E Television Networks, LLC*. Accessed January 8, 2015. http://www.history.com/topics/korean-war.

History Channel. "This Day in History, Aug. 8: 1974, Nixon Resigns." *A&E Television Networks, LLC*. Accessed June 16, 2015. http://www.history. com/this-day-in-history/nixon-resigns.

Hopkins, A.D. *The First 100: Portraits of Men and Women Who Shaped Las Vegas*, edited by K.J. Evans. Las Vegas: Huntington Press, 1999.

"How Does a Contingency Fee Agreement Work?" *FreeAdvice*. Accessed June 16, 2015. http://law.freeadvice.com/litigation/litigation/lawyer_contingency_fee.htm.

Hulse, Carl. "Harry Reid to Retire from Senate in 2016," *The New York Times*, March 27, 2015. http://www.nytimes.com/2015/03/28/us/politics/senator-harry-reid-retire.html.

"Jackie Robinson Biography," *A&E Television Networks, LLC.* Accessed February 12, 2012. http://www.biography.com/people/jackie-robinson-9460813#synopsis.

Kane, Paul. "Harry Reid to lay aside gloves, retire from Senate." *The Washington Post*, March 27, 2015. http://www.washingtonpost.com/politics/harry-reid-to-lay-aside-gloves-retire-from-senate/2015/03/27/07437f6e-d4c1-11e4-a62f-ee745911a4ff_story.html.

Kaplan, Rebecca. "Harry Reid Has Lost His Vision in His Right Eye," *CBS News*, April 8, 2015. http://www.cbsnews.com/news/harry-reid-has-lost-his-vision-in-his-right-eye/.

Kelly, Erin. "Analysts: 'Nuclear Option' Likely Won't Hurt Reid." *Reno-Gazette-Journal*, November 22, 2013.

Kelly, Erin. "Record Set for Longevity of Service," *Reno Gazette-Journal*, January 3, 2013.

Langley, Myrtle. "The Jewish Nation." *Eyewitness Religion, 46-51.* London: DK Publishing, 2012.

"Largest U.S. Churches, 2012." *Infoplease.* Accessed January 8, 2015. http://www.infoplease.com/world/religion/largest-us-churches.html.

Lowery, Wesley. "Harry Reid Sells Searchlight Home, Will Move Closer to Family in Vegas." *The Washington Post*, June 9, 2014. http://www.washingtonpost.com/blogs/post-politics/wp/2014/06/09/harry-reid-sells-searchlight-home-will-move-closer-to-family-in-las-vegas/.

Maloy, Simon. "Even More Serious Flaws Emerge in ASP Story About Reid's Attendance at Boxing Matches." *Media Matters for America*, May 31, 2006. http://mediamatters.org/research/2006/05/31/even-more-serious-flaws-emerge-in-ap-story-abou/135839.

Manning, Jennifer. "Membership of the 113th Congress: A Profile." *Congressional Research Service*. Last modified November 24, 2014. http://fas.org/sgp/crs/misc/R42964.pdf.

"Media Inquiries." *The University of Chicago Law School*. Accessed April 27, 2015. http://www.law.uchicago.edu/media.

Melton, John Gordon. "Mormon Religion." *Encyclopaedia Britannica*. Accessed June 8, 2015. http://www.britannica.com/topic/Mormonism.

Melton, John Gordon. "Nation of Islam." *Encyclopaedia Britannica*. Accessed April 27, 2015. http://www.britannica.com/EBchecked/topic/295614/Nation-of-Islam.

"Mining." *United States Senator for Nevada Harry Reid*. Accessed December 29, 2010. http://reid.senate.gov/index.cfm.

"Mormons in Congress 2012 – Final Results." *By Common Consent*, November 9, 2012. http://bycommonconsent.com/2012/11/09/mormons-in-congress-2012-final-results-2/.

"Muhammad Ali Biography." *A&E Television Networks, LLC*. Accessed June 9, 2015. http://www.biography.com/people/muhammad-ali-9181165.

"Muhammad Ali Biography." *Encyclopedia of World Biography*. Accessed April 27, 2015. http://www.notablebiographies.com/A-An/Ali-Muhammad.html.

"Muhammad Ali Biography." *Internet Movie Database*. Accessed April 27, 2015. http://www.imdb.com/name/nm0000738/bio.

"Muhammad Ali's Ring Record." *ESPN Classic*. November 19, 2003. http://espn.go.com/classic/s/Ali_record.html.

Myers, Dennis. "Citizen Reid." *Reno News & Review*, December 2, 2004. https://www.newsreview.com/reno/citizen-reid/content?oid=23692.

Myers, Dennis. "Harry Reid." *Online Nevada Encyclopedia*. October 14, 2010. http://www.onlinenevada.org/articles/harry-reid.

Nagourney, Adam. "Even in His Hometown, Reid is Source of Anguish." *The New York Times,* October 27, 2010. http://www.nytimes.com/2010/10/28/us/politics/28searchlight.html?_r=0.

Nagourney, Adam. "Reid Faces Battles in Washington and at Home." *The New York Times Magazine,* January 12, 2010. http://www.nytimes.com/2010/01/24/magazine/24reid-t.html?_r=0.

National Archives and Records Administration. "Constitution of the United States." *The Charters of Freedom "A New World Is At Hand."* May 23, 2015. http://www.archives.gov/exhibits/charters/constitution.html.

National Archives and Records Administration. "The Founding Fathers Delegates to the Constitution Convention." *The Charters of Freedom "A New World Is At Hand."* May 23, 2015. http://www.archives.gov/exhibits/charters/constitution_founding_fathers.html.

National Park Service. "Great Basin National Park." *National Park Service Land Resources Division Listing of Acreage (Summary).* Last modified December 31, 2011. https://irma.nps.gov/Stats/DownloadFile/107.

Natividad, Ivan V. "Harry Reid Meets Up with New Nationals." *Roll Call,* May 4, 2012. http://www.rollcall.com/news/Harry-Reid-Meets-Up-With-New-Nationals-Outfielder-214273-1.html.

"Negro League History 101." *NegroLeagueBaseball.com (P. Mills, publisher).* Accessed February 11, 2012. http://www.negroleaguebaseball.com/history101.html.

O'Callaghan, Mike. Forward to *Searchlight: The Camp That Didn't Fail* by Harry Reid, XI-XVII. Reno: University of Nevada Press, 1998.

O'Keefe, Ed. "Harry Reid Describes Exercise Injuries, Doesn't Rule Out Losing Sight in His Right Eye." *The Washington Post,* January 9, 2015. http://www.washingtonpost.com/blogs/post-politics/wp/2015/01/09/harry-reid-describes-exercise-injuries-doesnt-rule-out-losing-sight-in-his-right-eye/.

Passey, Brian. "Mormon Liberals: A 'Minority Within a Minority.'" *USA Today*, October 30, 2012. http://www.usatoday.com/story/news/politics/2012/10/30/mormon-liberals-minority/1669155/.

Peters, Jeremy W. "In Landmark Vote, Senate Limits Use of the Filibuster." *The New York Times*, November 21, 2013. http://www.nytimes.com/2013/11/22/us/politics/reid-sets-in-motion-steps-to-limit-use-of-filibuster.html?_r=0.

Polman, Dick. "Philadelphia Interview with Harry Reid About *The Good Fight: Hard Lessons from Searchlight to Washington*." *Free Library of Philadelphia*. Last modified May 9, 2008. http://libwww.freelibrary.org/authorevents/podcast.cfm?podcastID=94.

"Profiles and Contact Information for Members of the Senate in the 113th Congress." *U. S. Senate Profiles*. Accessed July 24, 2015. http://thatsmycongress.com/senate/113byalpha.html.

Rahman, Fazlur. "Islam." *Encyclopaedia Britannica*. Last modified June 17, 2015. http://www.britannica.com/topic/Islam.

Raju, Manu. "Harry Reid: Ritz-Carlton Not Home." *Politico*, October 21, 2010. http://www.politico.com/news/stories/1010/43989.html.

Ralston, Jon. "Harry Reid's Down, But Never Out." *Politico*, February 17, 2015. http://www.politico.com/magazine/story/2015/02/harry-reid-2016-jon-ralston-115234.html#.

Ralston, Jon. "Machiavelli With Malaprops." *Politico*, December 15, 2013. http://www.politico.com/magazine/story/2013/12/harry-reid-ralston-machiavelli-with-malaprops-101168.html#.

Rappeport, Alan. "Reid is Home after Surgery for Injuries." *The New York Times*, January 26, 2015. http://www.nytimes.com/2015/01/27/us/politics/reid-is-home-after-surgery-for-injuries.html?ref=topics&_r=0.

"Reid Given Top Award for Defending National Parks." Press Release. *United States Senator for Nevada Harry Reid*, April 2, 2009. http://www.reid.senate.gov/press_releases/reid-given-top-award-for-defending-national-parks

Reid, Harry. *The Good Fight: Hard Lessons From Searchlight to Washington.* New York: Berkley Books, 2008.

Reid, Harry. *Searchlight: The Camp That Didn't Fail.* Reno: University of Nevada Press, 1998.

"Reid Secures Nearly $14 Million in Education, Labor and Health Care Funding for Nevada." Press Release. *United States Senator for Nevada Harry Reid.* July 28, 2010. http://www.reid.senate.gov/press_releases/reid-secures-nearly-14-million-in-education-labor-and-health-care-funding-for-nevada.

Rindels, Michelle. "Sen. Reid Leaves Hospital after Vegas Car Crash." *Associated Press, AP Big Story*, October 27, 2012. http://www.bigstory.ap.org/article/sen-reid-taken-hospital-after-vegas-car-crash.

Roche, Lisa Riley. "Mormon Democrats Announce New National State Organizations." *Deseret News*, April 4, 2013. http://www.deseretnews.com/article/865577470/Mormon-Democrats-announce-new-national-state-organizations.html?pg=all.

Rodgers, Jane. "Joshua Trees." *National Park Service*, July 14, 2010. http://www.nps.gov/jotr/learn/nature/jtrees.htm.

Saxena, A. "Rheumatic Fever and Long-term Sequelae in Children." *Current Treatment Options in Cardiovascular Medicine*, 4, no. 4(2002): 309-319. Accessed April 21, 2015. http://www.ncbi.nlm.nih.gov/pubmed/12093388.

"School Meals." *United States Department of Agriculture (USDA) Food and Nutrition Service.* March 3, 2014. http://www.fns.usda.gov/school-meals/healthy-hunger-free-kids-act.

"Secretary Kempthorne Congratulates Senator Reid, Paiute Tribe, Federal and State Officials and Water Authority at Signing Ceremony for Truckee River Operating Agreement." News Release. *U.S. Department of the Interior.* November 9, 2008. http://www.doi.gov/news/archive/08_News_Releases/090808.html.

Senate Historical Office. "Senate History, 1878-1920: March 8, 1917 Cloture Rule." *United States Senate.* Accessed June 16, 2015. http://www.senate.gov/artandhistory/history/minute/Cloture_Rule.htm.

Senator Harry Reid. *United States Senator for Nevada Harry Reid.* Accessed December 15, 2013. http://www.reid.senate.gov/.

Smith, Christopher. "Senate's New Majority Whip: Senator Harry Reid of Nevada." *Salt Lake Tribune,* June 9, 2001. http://www.adherents.com/largecom/lds_Reid.html.

"Speleothems (Cave Formations)." Great Basin National Park Nevada. *National Park Service.* September 19, 2012. http://www.nps.gov/grba/learn/nature/speleothems-cave-formations.htm.

State of Nevada Legislative Counsel Bureau. "Office of Lieutenant Governor Audit Report." May 2, 2008. http://www.leg.state.nv.us/Division/Audit/Full/documents/OfficeofLieutenantGovernorLA08-18FULL.pdf.

Stein, Sam. "The Remarkable and Complex Legacy of One Harry Reid." *The Huffington Post,* March 27, 2015. http://www.huffingtonpost.com/2015/03/27/harry-reid-retires_n_6957414.html.

Steinhauer, Jennifer. "As Views Shift on Guns, Reid Corrals Senate." *The New York Times,* March 13, 2013. http://www.nytimes.com/2013/04/01/us/politics/harry-reid-draws-on-political-calculus-as-he-leads-senate.html?hp.

"Sudan: Death Toll in Darfur." *U.S. Department of State*. Accessed April 27, 2015. http://2001-2009.state.gov/s/inr/rls/fs/2005/45105.htm.

Taylor, Andrew. "Injuries Force Reid to Skip Opening Session of Senate." *The Washington Times*, January 6, 2015. http://www.washingtontimes. com/news/2015/jan/6/injuries-force-reid-to-skip-opening-session-of-sen/.

Terkel, Amanda. "Harry Reid Comes Out For Ban on Assault Weapons, High-Capacity Magazines." *Huff Post Politics*, April 17, 2013. http:// www.huffingtonpost.com/2013/04/17/harry-reid-assault-weap-ons-ban_n_3100164.html.

Tetreault, Steve. "Reid Says He Expects Recovery After Eye Surgery." *Las Vegas Review-Journal*, January 22, 2015. http://www.reviewjournal. com/politics/reid-says-he-expects-recovery-after-eye-surgery.

The Associated Press. "Senator Reid Admits Erring on Ethics Rule." *The New York Times*, June 2, 2006. http://www.nytimes.com/2006/06/02/ washington/02reid.html?_r=0.

The Center for Media and Democracy. "Harry Reid." *Source Watch: Your Guide to the Names Behind the News*. Last modified March 13, 2015. http://www.sourcewatch.org/index.php/Harry_Reid.

"The Truth about Lie Detectors (aka Polygraph Tests)." *American Psychological Association*. Accessed April 22, 2015. http://www.apa.org/re-search/action/polygraph.aspx.

Theobald, Bill. "Reid Still A Force." *USA Today*, November 16, 2014. http:// www.centralohio.com/usatoday/article/18548769.

Trickey, Eric. "Harry Reid." *Encyclopedia of World Biography*. Accessed August 8, 2013. http://www.notablebiographies.com/newsmakers2/2006-Ra-Z/Reid-Harry.html.

United States Senate. "March 8, 1917 Cloture Rule." *Senate History, 1878-1920*. Accessed June 16, 2015. http://www.senate.gov/artandhistory/history/minute/Cloture_Rule.htm.

Unnamed Reid staffer, interview with author, December 5, 2012.

U.S. Department of Justice, Bureau of Justice Statistics. "Domestic Violence/Abuse Statistics." *Statistic Brain Research Institute*. Last modified September 5, 2014. http://www.statisticbrain.com/domestic-violence-abuse-stats.

Virginia Gutenberg, telephone interview with author, March 3, 2015.

Waller, Doug. "Herding the Democrats." *Time*. November 14, 2004. http://content.time.com/time/magazine/article/0,9171,782108,00.html.

Walsh, Elsa. "Minority Retort: How a Pro-Gun, Anti-Abortion Nevadan Leads the Senate's Democrats." *The New Yorker*, August 8, 2005. http://www.newyorker.com/magazine/2005/08/08/minority-retort.

"What is a Seizure?" *Epilepsy Foundation*. Accessed April 22, 2015. http://www.epilepsy.com/learn/epilepsy-101/what-seizure.

"What We Do." *Nevada Legal Services*. Accessed June16, 2015. http://nlslaw.net/what-we-do/.

"What Harry Reid Said – and Reactions from Around the U.S." *Reno-Gazette-Journal*, March 27, 2015. http://www.rgj.com/story/news/2015/03/27/what-harry-reid-said-and-reactions/70537576/.

White, Ben. "Who'll Take the Reins from Harry Reid?" *CNBC*, March 27, 2015. http://www.cnbc.com/2015/03/27/wholl-take-the-reins-from-harry-reid.html.

"Where Did All the American Presidents Go to College?" *Success Degrees*. Accessed April 27, 2015. http://www.successdegrees.com/collegeeducationofamericanpresidents.html.

"World War II." *The Concise Columbia Encyclopedia, Second Edition*, 907-8. New York: Columbia University Press, 1989.

"Youth Central, Keeping the Door to College Open." *United States Senator for Nevada Harry Reid*. October 12, 2013. http://www.reid.senate.gov/services/youthcentral.

Zornick, George. "111th Congress Was Most Productive Session Since 'At Least' the 1960s." *Think Progress*, December 23, 2010. http://thinkprogress.org/politics/2010/12/23/136353/111-congress-achievement/.

PHOTO CREDITS

Figure 1: "Map of World's Largest Deserts." Public domain PNG image. WP-ClipArt.com, http://www.wpclipart.com/geography/world_maps/specialty/world_deserts.png.html (accessed April 1, 2015).

Figure 2: Richard Tropp. "Searchlight, Nevada." 2012. Photograph. Used with permission.

Figure 3: Ian Macky. "Map of Nevada (with Searchlight)." Copyright 2010, 2013. PAT Maps (public domain image). http://ian.macky.net/pat/map/us/nv/nv.html (accessed April 1, 2015).

Figure 4: Richard Tropp. Elementary school Reid attended, now a recreation center. November 2012. Used with permission.

Figure 5: Richard Tropp. The current Reid Elementary School in Searchlight, Nevada. November 2012. Used with permission.

Figure 6: The home where Harry Reid grew up. Photo courtesy of the Nevada Historical Society.

Figure 7: "Wounded soldiers in a trench." Photograph. ARC Identifier 195515. http://wwiiletters.blogspot.com (accessed April 1, 2015).

Figure 8: "U.S. soldiers take cover under fire somewhere in Germany." Photograph in the public domain. U.S. National Archive.

Figure 9: "U.S. Marines operating an M1919 A4 during World War II." Public domain image. http://firearmshistory.blogspot.com/2014_08_01_archive.html (accessed August 1, 2014).

Figure 10: Jurgen Stroop Report to Heinrich Himmler from May 1943. "Warsaw Ghetto Uprising." Original German caption reads: "Forcibly pulled out of dug-outs." Public Domain image. https://ezine.inverhills.edu/blog/why-i-teach-about-the-holocaust-photo-attributions/.

Figure 11: "Coutances, France: one of many destroyed towns." Public domain image. Wikimedia Commons. http://commons.wikimedia.org/wiki/File:WWII,_Europe,_Coutances,_France,_%22Once_there_was_a_church%22_-_NARA_-_196303.jpg (accessed April 1, 2015).

Figure 12: Charles Levy. "Mushroom cloud from the atomic explosion over Nagasaki at 11:02 a.m., August 9, 1945." Public domain image from Wikipedia.org. http://en.wikipedia.org/wiki/Nagasaki#/media/File:Nagasakibomb.jpg (accessed April 1, 2015).

Figure 13: "Nagasaki, Japan following the atomic bombing on August 9, 1945." Archive, Public domain image from Common Dreams Creative Commons Attribution-Share Alike 3.0 License http://commondreams.org/views/2014/08/07/war-crimes-nuclear-weaponry (accessed June 8, 2015).

Figure 14: Harry Reid, Sr. (age 2) in 1916 with family. Front (L-R): Joe Reid; Harry Reid, Sr.; Jeff Reid, Jane Reid. Middle (L-R): Mason Reid, John Reid, Harriet Reid, Robert Reid. Back (L-R): John's mother, Ellen Misener. Courtesy Searchlight Historical Museum.

Figure 15: "Jackie Robinson and Branch Rickey sign the contract that broke baseball's color barrier, August 28, 1945." Public domain image. Wikipedia.org. http://en.wikipedia.org/wiki/File:Robinson-contract.jpg (accessed April 1, 2015).

Figure 16: Bob Sandberg. "Robinson in Dodgers uniform, 1954." U.S. Library of Congress Prints and Photographs, digital ID ppm-sc.00047. Wikipedia.org. http://en.wikipedia.org/wiki/Jackie_Robinson_Day#/media/File:Jrobinson.jpg (accessed April 1, 2015).

Figure 17: "Jackie Robinson sliding onto base." Public domain image. BlackPast.org. www.blackpast.org/aaw/robinson-jack-jackie-roosevelt-1919-1972 (accessed April 1, 2015).

Figure 18: "Congressional Gold Medal awarded to Jackie Robinson." U.S. Mint Catalog. Public domain image. Wikipedia.org. http://en.wikipedia.org/wiki/File:2003_Jackie_Robinson_Congressional_Gold_Medal_front.jpg#/med (accessed April 1, 2015).

Figure 19: "The two Koreas, split at the 38th Parallel." Digital image in the public domain. Pixshark.com. Retrieved from http://pixshark.com/korean-war-38th-parallel.htm (accessed on April 10, 2015).

Figure 20: "United Nations' forces at the 38th Parallel, retreating back to the south from Pyongyang, in 1950." U.S. Federal Government photograph. Public domain. Retrieved from http://www.shmoop.com/korean-war/photo-38th-parallel.html (accessed on April 10, 2015)

Figure 21: "Pfc. Julias Van Den Stock of Company A, 32nd Regimental Combat Team, 7th Infantry Division, 1951." U.S. Government photograph. Public domain. Retrieved from http://commons.wikimedia.org/wiki/File:Korean_War_HA-SN-98-07010.jpg (accessed April 10, 2015)

Figure 22: "Men of the 1st Cavalry Division fighting in a train yard in Pyongyang, Korea." Public domain. Retrieved from http://usmilitary.about.com/library/milinfo/arhistory/nlkorea31.htm (accessed April 10, 2015).

Figure 23: Harry Reid in law school. *About Senator Harry Reid*. Retrieved from http://www.reid.senate.gov/about (accessed April 10, 2015).

Figure 24: Dave Parker. "Nevada Legislature Building, Carson City. Nov. 1, 2007." Used with permission through Creative Commons. Retrieved from http://commons.wikimedia.org/wiki/File:NevadaLegislatureBuilding.jpg (accessed April 21, 2015).

Figure 25: Lieutenant Governor Harry Reid. Photo courtesy of Nevada Historical Society. Used with permission.

Figure 26: "Muhammad Ali." Digital image in the public domain. Retrieved from http://www.blackpast.org/aah/ali-muhammad-1942 (accessed April 21, 2015).

Figure 27: Ira Rosenberg. "Portrait of Muhammad Ali, 1967." *World Journal Tribune* photo, U.S. Library of Congress. Image in the public domain. Retrieved from http://en.wikipedia.org/wiki/File:Muhammad_Ali_NYWTS.jpg (accessed April 21, 2015).

Figure 28: "Muhammad Ali (right) fights Joe Frazier." Image in the public domain. Retrieved from http://bmmphotopoetry.wordpress.com/2014/03/09/muhammad-alis-a-poet (accessed April 21, 2015).

Figure 29: "Rare bristlecone pine at Great Basin National Park." Digital image in the public domain. Retrieved from http://pixabay.com/en/great-basin-national-park-nevada-sky-80568/ (accessed April 27, 2015).

Figure 30: "Wheeler Peak, the tallest peak in Nevada, is inside Great Basin National Park." National Park Service photo, in the public domain. Retrieved from http://www.nps.gov/grba/photosmultimedia/index.htm (accessed April 27, 2015).

Figure 31: "Parachute Shield, the most famous shield in Lehman Caves." National Park Service, public domain image. Retrieved from http://www.nps.gov/media/photo/gallery.htm?id=1E0A1F74-155D-4519-3E89040C68F1098D (accessed April 27, 2015).

Figure 32: "Column and drapery formations found in Lehman Caves." National Park Service, public domain image. Retrieved from http://www.nps.gov/media/photo/gallery.htm?id=1E0A1F74-155D-4519-3E89040C68F1098D (accessed April 27, 2015).

Figure 33: "An abundance of speleothems are revealed in each room of Lehman Caves." National Park Service, public domain image. Retrieved from http://www.nps.gov/media/photo/gallery.htm?id=1E0A1F74-155D-4519-3E89040C68F1098D (accessed April 27, 2015).

Figure 34: "Helictites defying gravity, in the West Room of Lehman Caves." National Park Service, public domain image. Retrieved from http://www.nps.gov/media/photo/gallery.htm?id=1E0A1F74-155D-4519-3E89040C68F1098D (accessed April 27, 2015).

Figure 35: "Stalagmite ornately decorated in Lehman Caves." National Park Service, public domain image. Retrieved from http://www.nps.gov/media/photo/gallery.htm?id=1E0A1F74-155D-4519-3E89040C68F1098D (accessed April 27, 2015).

Figure 36: "A rare moment when water is forced under pressure through a soda straw formation." National Park Service, public domain image. Retrieved from http://www.nps.gov/media/photo/gallery.htm?id=1E0A1F74-155D-4519-3E89040C68F1098D (accessed April 27, 2015).

Figure 37: "On rare occasions, bubbles appear on soda straws for a short period of time, usually in early spring." National Park Service, public domain image. Retrieved from http://www.nps.gov/media/photo/gallery.htm?id=1E0A1F74-155D-4519-3E89040C68F1098D (accessed April 27, 2015).

Figure 38: "The emblem of the National Park Service." Digital image in the public domain. Retrieved from http://www.nps.gov/slbe/learn/education/classrooms/arrowhead.htm (accessed May 5, 2015).

Figure 39: "Scene at the Signing of the Constitution of the United States." Painting by Howard Chandler Christy. Digital image in the public domain. Retrieved from http://commons.wikimedia.org/wiki/File:Scene_at_the_Signing_of_the_Constitution_of_the_United_States.jpg (accessed May 5, 2015).

Figure 40: "Kids.gov Three Branches of Government Poster." 2014. U.S. General Services Administration, Federal Citizen Information Center, publication ID #6146. Retrieved from html://publications.usa.gov/USAPubs.php?PubID=6146 (accessed August 6, 2015).

Figures 41-47: Various pictures of Harry Reid throughout his career. Photos in the public domain, courtesy of Nevada Historical Society.

Figure 48: Senator Reid, at his Thursday Breakfast with the public. Photo by Adrienne Tropp, December 6, 2012.

Figure 49: "Senator Harry Reid meets with Julian Castro, nominee for Secretary of Housing and Urban Development, in July 2014." Retrieved from www.reid.senate.gov (accessed May 15, 2015).

Figure 50: "President Barack Obama talks with Senator Reid while on Air Force One." Digital image by White House Public Domain. Retrieved from www.acclaimimages.com/_gallery/_image_pages/0519-1010-0716-2846.html (accessed May 15, 2015).

Figure 51: Landra Reid. Public domain image courtesy of Nevada Historical Society.

Figure 52: "Harry and Landra Reid with their four sons and daughter." Retrieved from http://www.reid.senate.gov/about (accessed May 14, 2015).

INDEX

The letter *f* after a page number indicates an illustration.
HR refers to Harry Reid, Jr.

Adams, John, 96

Affordable Care Act (ACA), 113–14, 122–23

alcoholism

    among miners, 12

    of Harry Reid, Sr., 12–15, 22

    of Russell Payne, 64–69

Ali, Muhammad, 74–77, 76–77*f*

Allah, 75

Amendments to U.S. Constitution, 61, 89, 142

American Dream, viii, 141, 142

American League of Bicyclists, 104

American Recovery and Reinvestment Act, 114–15

Angle, Sharron, 124–26

Antifederalists, 142

Arrington, Leonard, 50

Articles of Confederation, 95–96, 142

assault weapons, 116

atomic bombs, 18, 20*f*

background checks, 83

Baker, Ross, 106

bar exam, 57–60

baseball, 22, 25–28, 34–35, 41

Basic High School, 20, 34–36, 39

bastards, 78

Bill of Rights, 142

bipartisanship, 125

Black Book, 83

Black Muslims, 75

Bolden, Larry, 63

bomb threats, 84

Bonaparte, Napoleon, 68

Boston Marathon, 39

boxing, 13, 36, 38–39, 45, 74–77, 103

breast cancer, 132–33

Briar, Bill, 80

bribery, 83–85

Brigham Young University, 135

Brown, Senator, 106

Brownback, Sam, 82

Bush, George H. W., 106

Bush, George W., 122

cancer stages, 133

Casino (movie), 82

casinos, 80–81, 82–85

Castro, Julian, 131*f*

caucus, 100, 138, 142

Cedar City, 43, 46

census, 143

children's obesity, 114

CHIP, 114

Church of Jesus Christ of Latter-day Saints. *See* Mormon Church

Clark County Hospital Board, 71

Clay, Cassius. *See* Ali, Muhammad

Clinton, Bill, 58

cloture rule, 128, 143

College of Southern Utah, 42, 43

Connecticut Compromise. *See* Great Compromise

constituents, 110–11, 143

Constitutional Convention of 1787, 96–97, 97*f*, 143

Darfur, 82

Daschle, Tom, 105

D-Day, 18

Deaner (drug in Payne case), 66–67

death threats, 82, 84, 137

Democratic National Committee, 79

Democratic Party, 71, 78–79, 90, 99–100, 102, 105–8, 113, 118–20, 124–25, 138–39, 143

deserts, 1–2, 1*f*

disabilities, 36

domestic violence (DV), 12–15

DUI (driving under the influence of alcohol), 64

Durban, Dick, 134

Durocher, Leo, 26

El Rey Motel, 6, 23–24

elections

    1974, 78–79

    1982, 89

1984, 90

1992, 99

1998, 99

2010, 109, 124–28

2012, 122

2014, 129–31

2016, 137

high school, 39

Ensign, John, 99, 117

entitlements, 143

epilepsy, 67–68

Equal Rights Amendment, 144

Ethics Committee, Senate, 102–3

executive branch of U.S. government, 96, 98*f*

extradition, 66–67, 144

federal boxing commission (proposed), 103

Federalists, 144

15th Amendment of U.S. Constitution, 89

filibusters, 127–28, 144

food costs (1960s vs. 2013), 59–60

football, 34, 41–42, 43

Ford, Gerald, 58, 79

Foreman, George, 75

Franklin, Benjamin, 96

Frazier, Joe, 75

Frome, Ted, 65

gaming world, 80, 82–85

gangsters, 80

Garrett Lee Smith Memorial Act, 115

General Mining Law of 1872, 117

George Washington University, 52

gold rush, 3

Golden Gloves, 74

The Good Fight (Reid), 13, 106

Gordon, Jack, 83–84

Gould, Earl, 42, 47–48, 60

Gould, Ruth, 42, 47

government shutdown, 128

grandfather clause, 144

Grant, Ulysses S., 94

Grateful Dead, 112

Great Basin National Park, 90–93*f*, 90–94

Great Compromise, 96, 143

guns, 116–17, 144

Gutenberg, Virginia, 34

Hamilton, Alexander, 96

hard rock mining. *See* mining

Hart, Mickey, 112

Hatch, Orrin, 100

Hayes, Rutherford B., 58

Healthy and Hunger-Free Kids Act, 114

Heller, Senator, 117

Henderson, Nevada, 6, 16, 20–22, 29–30, 33, 43–44, 46–47, 60, 134

Herzik, Eric, 129

Hitler, Adolf, 17

Holmes, Larry, 75

The Holocaust, 17

Hunt, Lorraine, 39

ideology, 144
illegitimate children, 78
impeachment, 79
incumbent, 144
Independent (politician), 145
integration, 25–28
IOUs, 129–30
Iraq War, 121
Islam, 75

jackrabbit stew, vii–viii, 141
Judaism, 47
Judd, Harmon, 50
judicial branch of U.S. government, 96, 98*f*
Julius Caesar, 68
juries, 62–63

Kempthorne, Dirk, 99
Kennedy, Ted, 122
Korean conflict, 37–38, 37–38*f*

Las Vegas Review-Journal, 122
lawmaking process, 109. *See also* legislation
lawyers, 61–62
Laxalt, Paul, 79
Legal Services Corporation (LSC), 61
legislation, viii, 90, 117, 127, 145. *See also* lawmaking process
legislative branch of U.S. government, 96, 98*f*, 145. *See also* U.S. Congress

Lehman Caves, 90–93, 90–93*f*

Leonardo da Vinci, 68

liberals, 125

lie detectors, 66

lieutenant governor, 73

Lincoln, Abraham, 9, 94

Liston, Sonny, 75–76

lobbyists, 103–4, 117, 145

Logan, Utah, 49–50

Lokken, Fred, 129–30

MacArthur, Douglas, 37

Madison, James, 68, 96

Major League Baseball, 25–28

majority leader
   HR as, viii, 105–11, 130, 145
   Mitch McConnell as, 129

majority rule, 145

manslaughter, 69

marathons, 39

Mariposa Grove of Giant Sequoias, 94

Martello, Willie, 23–24

Martinez, Rey, 35, 39

mass shootings, 116

McConnell, Mitch, 100, 108, 129

mezuzah, 48

Michelangelo, 68

mining, 3, 11, 16, 21–22, 117

minority leader, 105, 108–9, 129–30

Mormons and Mormon Church, 35–36, 48, 49–50, 53, 100, 119–20, 135

Mr. Cleanface, 84–85

Muhammad, Elijah, 75

musical therapy, 112

Nagourney, Adam, 30, 107

Nation of Islam (NOI), 75

National Park Service (NPS), 95, 95*f*

National Park System, 90–95, 95*f*

National Rifle Association (NRA), 104, 116

Negro League baseball, 25–26

Nevada Athletic Commission, 103

Nevada Check Up, 114

Nevada Gaming Commission, 80–81, 82–85

Nevada Legal Services, 61–62

Nevada State Legislature, 71–72, 72*f*

9/11 terrorist attacks, 140

19th Amendment of U.S. Constitution, 89, 145

Nixon, Richard, 58, 78–79

nuclear option, 127

nuclear waste, 106

Obama, Barack, 58, 82, 106–8, 113, 121–22, 131*f*, 138, 140

Obama, Michelle, 114

Obamacare, 113–14

obesity, 114

O'Callaghan, Mike

    boxing and, 36, 38–39

    college scholarship for HR and, 42

    as governor of Nevada, 73, 78, 80

    on HR, 63, 100

as inspiration to HR, 71

loans HR money, 59

as mentor to HR, 50–51, 52, 141

Older Americans Act, 112

112th Congress, 108

Paine, Pop, 28

Paiute Indian Tribe, 98–99

party whips, 102, 146

Payne, Emmalyn, 64–70

Payne, Martin, 64–70

Payne, Russell, 64–70

Pearl Harbor, 17

political parties, 73, 99–100, 107–8, 145. *See also* Democratic
  Party; Republican Party

polygraph tests, 66

primary elections (primaries), 99, 124–25, 145

pro bono, 62

Quarry, Jerry, 74–75, 77

radio, 10, 25

Ralston, Jon, 105–6, 108, 138

Reconnecting Homeless Youth Act, 114

Reid, Dale, 5, 20, 29, 78

Reid, Don, 5, 20, 22, 29, 78

Reid, Harriet, vii–viii, 112

Reid, Harry, Jr., 53*f*, 54*f*, 130–31*f*

  baseball and, 22, 25–28, 34–35, 41

  birth of, 5, 78

  boxing and, 13, 36, 38–39, 45, 74–77, 103

bribery and, 83–85

character of, 10, 28, 100

childhood home of, 8–10, 9*f*

childhood of, vii–viii, 5–11, 8–9*f*, 12–15, 16–22, 23–24, 25–30

children of, 50, 78, 135, 135*f*

as city attorney in Henderson, 60–61

as Clark County Hospital Board of Directors chair, 71

criticism of, 108–9, 124–28, 139

death and bomb threats against, 84

drinking, attitude toward, 15

education of, 7–8, 8*f*, 28–29, 33–42, 43–44, 49–50, 57–60

elections and. *See* elections

employment, college, 46

employment, youthful, 22, 40

eye injury of, 33, 134

father's death, 77–78

football and, 22, 34, 41–42, 43

health issues and injuries of, 33, 40–41, 132–34

illegitimacy of, 78

interests of, personal, 136

as lawyer in Las Vegas, 61–63, 64–70

leadership skills of, 105–6, 129–30, 138, 140

as marathon runner, 39

marriage of. *See* Reid, Landra (née Gould)

mayor of Las Vegas campaign, 78–80

as miner, 22

(mis)statements of, 121–23

money problems of, 52–53

in movies, 82

murder case of Russell Payne and, 64–70

as Nevada assemblyman, 71–72

as Nevada Gaming Commission chair, 80–81, 82–85

as Nevada lieutenant governor, 73–74, 73*f*

nickname of, 34

parents of. *See* Reid, Harry, Sr.; Reid, Inez

politics of, as senator, 112, 113–15, 116–20

private lifestyle of, 136

religion of, 35–36, 49, 53, 119–20

retirement of, 138–39

as Senate Democratic Whip, 102

as Senate Ethics Committee chair, 102–3

Senate Ethics Committee investigation of, 103

as Senate majority leader, viii, 105–11, 113, 130

as Senate minority leader, 129–31

student government and, 39, 46

success and importance of, 140–41

as U.S. Capitol Police officer, 52

as U.S. congressman, 89–94

as U.S. senator, 94, 98–101, 124–28, 129–31

youthful pranks of, 23–24, 46

Reid, Harry, Sr., 21*f*

alcoholism of, 12–15, 22

birth of Harry, Jr., 5

death of, 77–78

dental problems of, 5–6

domestic violence and, 12–15

mining accident of, 11

occupations of, 3, 10–11, 16, 21–22, 34

Reid, Inez, 5–6, 10–11, 12–14, 28–29, 41

Reid, Jane, 21

Reid, Joe, 21, 21*f*, 35

Reid, Josh, 78

Reid, Lana, 50, 132

Reid, Landra (née Gould), 133*f*

    background of, 42

    car bomb and, 84

    children of, 50, 78, 135, 135*f*

    education of, 43–44

    encourages HR to stay in law school, 52–53

    health issues and injuries of, 132–33

    interests of, personal, 136

    marriage to HR, 48

    private lifestyle of, 136

    religion of, 47–48, 49, 53

    in Searchlight, 29–30

Reid, Larry, 5, 10

Reid, Ray, 21, 21*f*, 35

Reid Elementary School, 8*f*

"Reid Faces Battles in Washington and at Home" (Nagourney), 107

Republican Party, 99–101, 102, 105–8, 113, 118–20, 124, 127, 129, 139, 145

rheumatic fever, 40–41

Rickey, Branch, 26, 27*f*

Robinson, Dorothy, 41

Robinson, Jackie, 25–28, 27–28*f*

Romney, Mitt, 122

Roosevelt, Theodore, 68

Sand and Sorrow (movie), 82

Sandoval, Brian, 137, 139

Sandy Hook Elementary School, 116

Schumer, Chuck, 100

Searchlight, Nevada
    as HR's childhood home, 1–4, 2*f*, 5–7, 21–22, 23–24
    as HR's future burial place, 30
    as HR's part-time home, 29–30, 33–35, 48, 112
    map of, 7*f*
    schools in, 8*f*
Searchlight Cemetery, 30
Searchlight: The Camp That Didn't Fail (Reid), 29
Second Amendment of U.S. Constitution, 61
segregation, 25–28, 74
seniority, 129, 145
separation of powers, 96–98, 146
Smith, Joseph, 36
Social Security Act, 112, 146
Social Security Retirement Benefits, 112
Spinks, Leon, 75
Stein, Sam, 140
streptococcus, 40–41
Sudan, 82
suicide, 77, 115
supermajority, 127–28

Taft, William, 58
Tea Party, 124–25, 146
Texas Rangers, 85
Theobald, Bill, 129
Traffic (movie), 82
Tribal Courts, 62
Truman, Harry, 37
truth serum, 68–69

United States Capitol Police, 52

University of Nevada, Las Vegas (UNLV), 43

U.S. Capitol Visitor Center, 121

U.S. Congress, 37, 57–58, 61, 72, 89–90, 95–97, 102–4, 143.
See also U.S. House of Representatives; U.S. Senate

U.S. Constitution, 89, 97*f*

U.S. government, branches of, 98*f*

U.S. House of Representatives, 85, 89–94, 96, 98*f*, 108, 120

U.S. Senate, 89, 96, 98–101, 98*f*, 102–4, 105–11, 120, 124–28

Utah State University, 49–51

V-E Day, 18

Vietnam War, 76

vouchers, 112, 146

washday, 10

Washington, George, 96–97

Watergate scandal, 78–79

White House, 95

Whittemore, Harvey, 126

Wilson, Woodrow, 94, 127–28

women and work, 50–51

World War II, 16–20, 18–20*f*, 51

Yellowstone National Park, 4–95

Yosemite Valley, 94

Young Democrats, 46

Youth Central Page, 111

Yucca Mountain, 106, 117

ABOUT THE AUTHOR

ADRIENNE TROPP has been a political junkie since probably the age of five. She listened intently to discussions by her family and neighbors, and as a young teenager began expressing her views to others. In college, she took a more active part in politics: She dispersed campaign literature, knocked on people's doors, and did telephone canvassing. Her goal was often to get out the vote.

When she met her husband, Richard Tropp, she found a like-minded soul, so her interest in politics never waned. Their son and daughter, not surprisingly, grew up in a household filled with political debate.

Adrienne has taught in New York, Texas, North Carolina, and Nevada, the four states in which she's lived. She has always believed students should not know their teachers' political views. She is proud that her students rarely figured out whom she was supporting in an election.

After retiring from teaching, Adrienne ran a tutoring service, undertook her dream of writing, and found time for traveling. Perhaps her newest loves, her grandchildren, may supplant politics in her heart.